The

GRASMERE,

5.7.'86

d. G. Tooley

Thirlmere, modified by the hand of man (Drive 2)

The Lakes

Brian Knapp

Illustrations by Duncan McCrae and Brian Knapp

London
GEORGE ALLEN & UNWIN
Boston   Sydney

George Allen & Unwin (Publishers) Ltd,
40 Museum Street, London WC1A 1LU, UK

George Allen & Unwin (Publishers) Ltd,
Park Lane, Hemel Hempstead, Herts HP2 4TE, UK

Allen & Unwin Inc.,
9 Winchester Terrace, Winchester, Mass 01890, USA

George Allen & Unwin Australia Pty Ltd,
8 Napier Street, North Sydney, NSW 2060, Australia

First published in 1984

ISSN 0265–3117

Sketch-maps on pp. 48, 56, and 64 based in part on Ordnance Survey
mapping: Crown Copyright reserved.

British Library Cataloguing in Publication Data

Knapp, Brian
    The Lakes. – (Unwin countryside guides ; 1)
1. Lake District (England) – Description
and travel – Guide-books
I. Title
914.27'804858   DA670.L1
ISBN 0–04–551083–0

Set in 9 on 10 point Palatino by Nene Phototypesetters, Northampton
and printed in Hong Kong by Colorcraft Ltd

Contents

Introduction: getting away from it all

> Here among the mountains, our curiosity was frequently moved
> to enquire what hill this was, or that. Indeed, they were in my
> thoughts, monstrous high; but in a country all mountainous and
> full of innumerable high hills, it was not easy for a traveller to
> judge which was the highest.
>
> Daniel Defoe, *c*.1724.

There can scarcely be anyone who has driven along the M6 who has
not been drawn by those evocative words, 'The Lakes'. Each year
millions slip from the monotonous motorway into the magic of the
Lake District. The Lake District is rather special, not least because it is
actually a region of mountains and lakes. You can find mountains
galore in Scotland, and large lakes in many parts of Britain, but here
mountains, lakes and sea are side by side. High mountains provide a
dramatic backdrop to the lakes, which highlight the drama of the
mountains. Both lakes and mountains are manageable – you do not
get lost among them, nor are you dwarfed by them; you can easily
walk up most of the fells (mountains) or around a water (lake); and
from the top of the higher fells you can see the surrounding plain and
the Irish Sea.

What is more, despite the great influx of visitors, Lakeland seems to
be able to contain them all without bursting at the seams. True, the
main roads are congested at the height of summer, but everyone is
free to leave their cars and venture just a few steps up the fellsides or
beside a lake shore. There all can enter a world of rare peace and tranquillity. Here in this guide, you will find a selection of routes that will
help you to understand a little better how Lakeland scenery has
evolved, and so increase your enjoyment of a wonderful part of
Britain as you get away from it all.

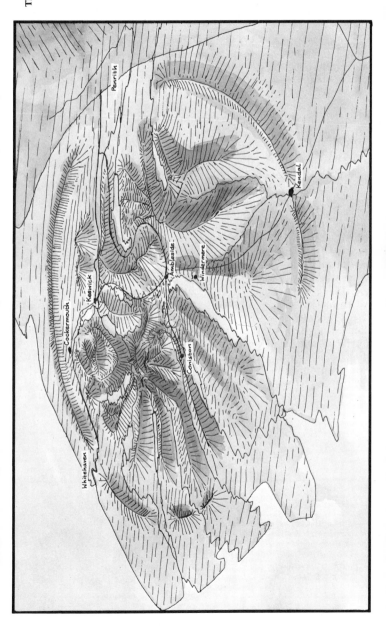

Key to symbols

☕	café
🅿	car park
🏰	castle, abbey, stately home, etc.
🚗	motor route
M	museum, gallery, exhibition, etc.
PO	post office
🍺	public house
🚂	railway
🛍	shop
[Skiddaw >]	signpost
✆	telephone
WC	toilet
ℹ	tourist information
✲	viewpoint
🚶	walking route

RED DEER

This is the largest native deer. It is particularly common in Scotland but you may also catch a glimpse of this majestic animal in Lakeland. Usually, these shy animals reveal their presence only by their hoofprints (left), which are about twice the size of those of sheep (right).

PART 1 BACKGROUND

You may enjoy the landscape for the beauty of its form, the patch-work colours of its fells, or the cooling breezes that waft in from its lakes. But you can hardly stay in Lakeland for long before you begin to wonder how the lakes were formed, or why some mountains are rugged and others more rounded, or even why there should be mountains at all. Furthermore, the pretty stone-built hamlets and twisting narrow roads invite you to ask why they should be at those chosen spots, or why walls follow particular lines across the land-scape. The more you look, the more questions spring to mind. In the pages that follow, we will provide some of the answers. Because man arrived on the Lakeland scene relatively recently in its history, we shall turn first to the slow development of the *natural* landscape.

SHELDUCK

This distinctive bird of estuary muds and marshes is intermediate in size between ducks and geese. Much of its plumage is a striking white, but it has a dark band across the back of the wings, a chestnut-coloured breast band, a green head and a red bill. When not waddling around in the mud and dipping into pools, it is often seen rump up as it searches for food while swimming in shallow water.

The countryside as it was

In the beginning

If you visit Lakeland over a period of many years, you begin to remember the form of the landscape, the position of unusual stones in the bed of a stream, the shape of a river bank. The more years you visit, the more you will notice that the stones gradually move, swept onwards by each year's floods, or that the river slowly alters course and cuts nearer to your path. These are only small changes, but that is how the landscape evolves. Most landscapes are in no hurry to develop, and Lakeland is one of the oldest and most slowly changing of all.

There was a time, over 600 million years ago, when Lakeland did not exist at all. Where the peaks of Scafell now stand and the great bulk of Skiddaw rears up against the sky, there was nothing but a vast ocean. Silt and clay, washed down by rivers from far-away mountains, slowly settled out over the sea bed, building grain upon grain, layer upon layer. For over a hundred million years a huge thickness of these muds was built up, until slowly an important change overtook the region. The ocean that had once been so wide became narrower as continents slowly drifted across the face of the Earth on a collision course. Now the peace and tranquillity of the deep ocean was disappearing, and in its place arose a land wracked by earthquakes and shot through with volcanoes sending searing hot clouds of ash up through the water and high into the sky – an underwater Mount St Helens on a grand scale.

At this time, Lakeland was simply a line of volcanic islands that had forced their way upwards through the sea bed. Towering volcanoes of ash and lava would have reared up sending ashes far and wide, which settled back gradually into the waters, adding to the muds brought from the nearby continent. At the same time, fiery tongues of white-hot lava were thrust from below into the old ocean muds. These pushed the layers apart before finally cooling as sheets of rock called sills, or cutting through them to make walls of lava, which later solidified as dykes.

This period lasted perhaps for another 100 million years, during which time there were many stupendous eruptions and violent earthquakes. When the ashes and lavas of these ancient volcanoes were finally cooled and compacted, they had become tough rocks that, later, were well able to withstand the effects of the agents of erosion. These are the rocks that today make the bold craggy forms of the central fells, of Great Gable, of the Langdale Pikes and of Scafell itself.

A quiet phase followed, in which more muds and sands were laid down. Then, literally, came the final crunch. For over a hundred million years the old ocean had been growing smaller and smaller; now it was disappearing completely, crushed between the irresistible jaws of the slowly moving continents that were ultimately to become

welded together. The crunch was mighty and long. The ocean bed was crushed and torn, its rocks jolted and jostled. The muds folded into tightly contorted forms; the ashes and lavas, being more resistant, folded less severely or just broke into pieces along huge tear (or fault) lines. Wherever one piece of ocean floor was wrenched past another, it was shattered and smashed into countless fragments; wherever it was upfolded, it became bent and then cracked into blocks resembling the lintel stones over an arch. At the end, the whole crumpled and contorted mass was pushed bodily skywards so that the ocean floor became giant mountains. Lakeland had been born.

Nevertheless, the growth of the mountains was far from over, for deep within the Earth huge bubbles of molten granite began to rise into the mountain core, gradually moving upwards until finally they shed their heat to the rock around and solidified. In this way Lakeland acquired a true heart of stone, a core of massive granite that is now visible through 'windows' in the cover rock between Shap Fell in the east and Eskdale in the west. While the granite was still molten, boiling liquids flowed out, pushing their way into the cracked rocks above, cooling and solidifying as veins of metal ore for which man was later to rip the mountainsides apart.

The genesis of Lakeland began like a lamb and finished like a lion. It was followed by a hundred million years of quiet conditions. During this time, the elements of the weather began patiently to dismantle the mountains pebble by pebble, grain by grain. Rain and frost, flood and landslide wore the mountains down to hills, then to plains, until finally the once-giant mountains were no more. Over this land a new ocean gradually spread, this time warm and teeming with sufficient life to build vast reefs of coral and create thick beds of limy mud. These thick beds were to become the limestone hills that now stretch in a ring around the perimeter of the main Lakeland peaks. Then, once more, conditions changed, and limy muds became dry land, this time in a climate whose searing heat and scorching winds deposited sand dunes across barren deserts not unlike those of the Sahara today. Occasionally, the sea flooded over this desert land, dumping red muds on the sand dunes; but it always evaporated away again, leaving white beds of sparkling salt. For millions of years such conditions prevailed and the bright red rocks of St Bees began to form. Then, slowly, the climate changed again, turning desert into tropical rainforest swamp. Where sand dunes once dominated, giant trees now flourished, died and were buried amid the sands and muds of vast deltas. Under these tropical deltas great changes were also occurring. As water seeped down through the desert sands, it washed the red iron stain into the limy mud beneath, where it remained, trapped underneath what was later to become Egremont, until the hand of man dug it from the Earth as iron ore nearly 300 million years later.

However, it was not quiet for long. Just after the coal seams were formed from the decayed trees amid a mass of delta sands, the area was wracked once more by terrifying violence. Earthquake after

The countryside as it was 5

earthquake must have shaken the land as forces within the crust slowly heaved Lakeland into a great dome-shaped mountain range, and at the same time wrenched it clear from the land of the Pennines to the east. Now, for the first time, the broad bulk of Lakeland stood alone, although its shape was still very far from that which we see today. Once more, ice and water erosion chiselled and ground at the rocks, this time flowing radially outwards from the centre of the dome, gradually stripping off the coal seams, then the desert sandstone, and finally the limestone, until they were left merely as low encircling ridges, their eroded faces turned towards the mountains they had once covered.

From that time onwards, Lakeland has stood proud of its surroundings, gradually reducing its stature by the unceasing efforts of ice and water. Slowly the heart of the old mountain chain has been revealed: today, the ancient mudstones, the volcanic ashes, the lava and the granite core are all laid bare.

The age of ice

Geological events in the distant past remain evident only as shadows, and the landscape today only hints at what the area was like aeons ago. More recent events are far clearer. The final chapter in the natural shaping of the British Isles, the Ice Age, has been largely responsible for moulding the landscape into fells and dales.

About 2 million years ago – a brief span in Lakeland's history – the fells were smooth and rounded, their summits covered with soil and vegetation, their slopes thickly mantled in forest. Even Scafell was like this. Most striking of all, however, there were no lakes. Then something dramatic happened. Quite rapidly the climate became much cooler and the forest died. Lakeland had entered the Ice Age. As southwesterly winds brought snows off the Atlantic, hollows in hillsides facing the sheltered north-east were filled up with drifting snow. Slowly but surely, snow piled upon snow until eventually, after many hundreds of years, it compacted into ice and the first glaciers were created. Just as water had once gathered into the hollows to form streams, so ice moved under its own weight, slipping and sliding over the soil, tearing it away until the bare rock was exposed beneath. Ice behaves very differently from running water, since it cannot twist and turn around every obstacle as streams do. Instead it simply pushes ahead, using its weight to smash and grind a way through the landscape. In the same way as the stonemason's mallet and chisel chip off pieces of rock, and his file applies the final smooth finish to his work, so ice cut into the Lakeland stone, chipping away blocks from the solid rock. These blocks froze fast to the undersurface of the ice so that, as it slid down slope, they were scraped across fellside and valley floor like a giant file. Sometimes the teeth of the file were fine and only a rounded and smooth surface was left behind; at other times large lumps of rock, sometimes as large as a house, were dragged across the landscape, gouging great scratch

(Opposite) **Great Gable 500 million years ago** (USGS photo)

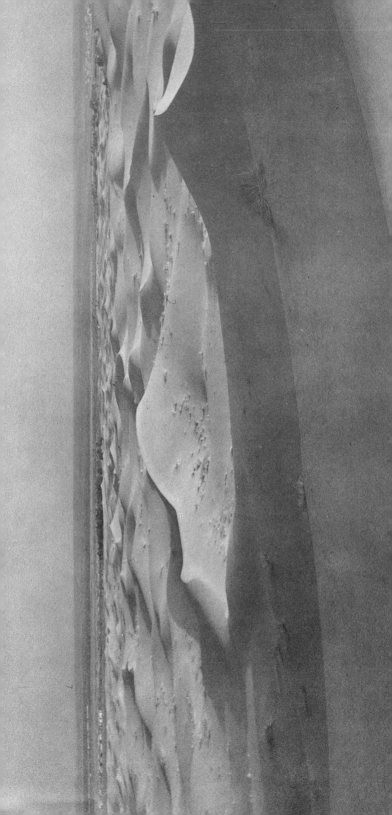

marks that remain fresh today. High above the ice on the windswept summits, where there was little permanent snow and the land was exposed to harsh weather, intense frosts shattered rocks into sharp-edged fragments, which then fell away, thereby honing the landscape into the crags that now lure the climber.

Thus, as ice spilled from its fellside hollows, enormous quantities of rock were chipped and scraped away, finally transforming the gentle hollows into deep, bowl-shaped features that today hold some of Lakeland's most beautiful small tarns (round lakes). Harrop Tarn above Thirlmere (Walk 6), Red Tarn below Helvellyn's summit, and many others, were formed this way.

Dramatic as this early erosion was, the formation of the deep hillside hollows (known in Lakeland as combes and coves) was only just beginning. As ice spilled from the pitted mountainside down into the valleys, it tore and crushed the rock with even greater force. It bit deep into the soft rock, and even ground its way downwards through the toughest rocks Lakeland had to offer, until the V-shaped slope profiles of the river valleys had been bulldozed and replaced by the deep, wide and straight troughs that are the dales we know today. However, ice is a solid: apply pressure in one place and the whole mass moves. So, as snow accumulated in the highest parts of the fells, the glaciers in the valleys below responded like toothpaste being squeezed out of a tube. Pushed on by the weight of the snow from behind, glaciers even defied gravity by moving up hill. Wherever a band of tough rock held up the rate of erosion, the glaciers simply overrode it, at the same time biting deeply into the softer rocks on either side. In this way, the evenly sloping river valleys were transformed into a series of long basins separated by ridges of more-resistant rock; most of today's lakes now lie in these basins.

Within these valleys, erosion proceeded apace, obeying the harsh rule of 'survival of the fittest'. Thus, large glaciers cut down quickly

Volcanic rock moulded and scratched by ice

A frost-shattered granite boulder

(Opposite) **Harrop Tarn in early Ice Age times**

Scafell in mid Ice Age times

into the floors of large valleys, whereas smaller glaciers cut more slowly. Some small glaciers were even blocked completely by major ice streams so that they could not move at all. As a result, in many a small valley, erosion ceased altogether, and today such valleys appear much as they did before the ice came. The sites of these important glaciers can be seen because their valleys have been left hanging high above the trench-like valleys cut by their larger neighbours. The difference in height is highlighted by many of Lakeland's most delicate waterfalls. Taylorgill Force (Walk 4), the Lodore Falls in Borrowdale (Walk 3), and Aira Force beside Ullswater (Walk 7) all fall from small hanging valleys.

This was also the time when some glaciers were able to bite so deeply into the fellsides that all they left were long knife-edge ridges, such as the famous Striding Edge on Helvellyn. However, most glaciers were not powerful enough to erode the broad backs of the fells in this way, and these remain as wide, rounded crests.

As the grip of the Ice Age tightened, the effects of the ice changed. After a while, even the largest glaciers were blocked as they pushed through into the lowland, for here they met huge ice sheets spreading southeastwards from Scotland. In effect, Lakeland was at this time an island of mountain glaciers hemmed in by an ocean of thick lowland ice. Without an easy means of escape, Lakeland ice piled ever higher in its valleys until it began spilling out over the lowest parts of the valley walls, scraping and tearing at the rock until the walls were breached. This is how the many passes such as Sty Head and Dunmail Raise were born. For man, these glacial breaches have been the most important developments of all, because without them there would be little chance of crossing the fells. For example, the breach at Dunmail

(Opposite) **Ullswater from the north as it might have looked in Ice Age times, with Kirkstone Pass in the distance and Fairfield fell in the right centre**

Raise provides the only direct route connecting Keswick to Ambleside and Kendal (Drive 2).

These early stages of glacial activity created the steepest and most spectacular parts of the Lakeland landscape. However, as Lakeland ice remained largely a prisoner in its own mountains, it piled up until the whole region became buried, leaving only the highest peaks standing proud. At the height of the Ice Age, the area must have looked much as Greenland does today. If ice had always been confined to the valleys, and if ice in the combes had had the time to erode more deeply, the Lakeland landscape would probably have been transformed into sharp and jagged peaks like the Alps, and Scafell might well have been a British Matterhorn. As it was, ice buried this type of landscape in its infancy and left us with the more rounded summits seen today.

Glaciers overwhelmed Lakeland for hundreds of thousands of years, yet only about 12 000–15 000 years ago the ice began to melt quickly away. Nevertheless, the effects of glaciation were not over, for the ice carried a sting in its tail.

Melting rapidly, the ice yielded vast amounts of water, yet still remained obstinately filling the valley bottoms. Some of this water gushed along the sides of the glaciers, cutting channels deeply into the fellside; the rest tumbled down crevasses in the surface of the ice and finally found its way to the valley floor. This water could not flow freely, because it was confined by ice above and on both sides. It therefore flowed within an ice tunnel, rushing and tumbling along and using some of the glacial debris to cut deep trenches into the valley floors.

Eventually the ice disappeared and water began to flow freely across the valley floors once more. These were not the valleys of the rivers before the Ice Age; their floors had been scoured, widened and deepened into basins where the soft rock had once been. Into these basins poured the waters from melting glaciers, filling them to produce the beautiful lakes we see today. When they had been filled, they overflowed, linking the lakes with the clear waters of little rivers and cascading over the steep steps where tougher rock remained.

The melting ice released not only water but also millions of tons of debris scraped from the fells and the valleys. No longer trapped in its icy prison, the chaos of boulders and clay (termed 'boulder clay') was left plastered over the valley sides or in great piles on the valley floors like so much rubbish.

Twelve thousand years may seem a long time but, since the ice finally vanished, there has been relatively little time for today's rivers to alter the scene. They have picked at the glacial rubbish in places, carrying the clay away and dumping it in the lakes; but, as boulder-strewn river beds still show, today's streams are no match for glaciers when it comes to transporting larger stones. Do not imagine that the streams of modern Lakeland have transported all the boulders that litter their channels or that they have formed the valleys all around, for they have barely started reshaping the valleys. Today's landscape is still very much the work of the ice.

(Opposite) **Boulders and clay (3, Walk 4)**

The countryside today

The Lakeland landscape has evolved over 600 million years of fashioning by enormous forces within the Earth and ceaseless erosion by water and ice. By chance we see it almost immediately after an ice age has departed. The wide, overdeepened valleys forming the floors of the lakes will surely be filled in and the boulder clay will be washed away. For now, however, the boulder clay remains as the foundation of soils on the valley floors and out on the plains. Small valleys still hang as sites for waterfalls to delight the eye, and frost still sharpens the fellsides and litters the lower slopes with screes, but the lakes will not last for ever. Derwentwater has already been separated from Bassenthwaite. Crummock Water is now separated from Buttermere by material brought down by rivers, and both lakes owe much of their irregular shorelines to similar, if smaller, infilling by numerous small streams. Eventually all the lakes will be filled in completely as the remaining glacial debris is swept off the fellsides by the cascading streams. Likewise some of the screes are already weathering into soil and being covered with vegetation. In a few tens of thousands of years – a brief period of geological time – all the crags will be gone, as rivers and soils once more take command. No landscape remains the same for ever.

Because Lakeland has so recently been released from the clutches of the ice, the landscape we see today is more varied than at any other time in its long history; yet, in essence, it is a very simple guidebook to all who have the time and inclination to stop to read it. For example,

A knob of glacially scoured rock provides a vantage point to Wastwater's famous screes

Buttermere (foreground) is separated from Crummock Water by a large delta of material washed down from Sail Beck (right): Drive 3 follows the road seen at right; Walk 5 provides the viewpoint ()

the ancient ocean muds, long folded and crushed, are still easily distinguished as broad rounded fells. In these easily eroded rocks, no steep-sided hollow or crag could survive for long. Only where the 'slates' are cut by tough dykes and sills (Walk 1) do these landscapes show any enduring sharpness of form. By contrast, the volcanic rocks of the central fells, although varying considerably in character, are tough and stand rugged and proud against the sky. Their east-facing sides are pitted with glacially scoured hollows, and their valleys are deep and steep sided.

The countryside today 17

Beyond these mountain areas are more subdued fells. Those south of Coniston are made largely from the same mudstone and shale rocks as Skiddaw, whereas others are of granite. However, granite does not form the most prominent ground as it does on Dartmoor. In Lakeland, granite creates rather subdued fells because it is only just emerging from beneath a cover of other rocks. Beyond all these 'inner' fells come the encircling rings of grey limestone, yellow coal-bearing sandstone, and finally red sandstone that make the lower country from which Lakeland rises majestically.

And then came man

Why should people want to inhabit a range of formidable mountains when there was so much inviting lowland nearby? The simple answer is that men who arrived after the Ice Age did not see the landscape as we do today, and the weather was very different too. Curiously, within a couple of thousand years of the retreat of the ice, the climate was much warmer and drier than it is today.

Stone Age man found Lakeland covered with trees – oak, ash, birch, hazel and alder – stretching from the valley bottom up to 2500 ft (762 m). Like his contemporaries elsewhere in Britain, he shunned the densely wooded and marshy valley bottoms and headed for the hills, where trees were less massive and more easily chopped down. So he went up into the Lakeland fells, first in search of game, and later for a place to clear ground and grow his crops. The felled trees were used for making shelter and for heating and cooking; bark was used for waterproofing, perhaps even for dinner-plates! The tough volcanic rocks yielded a stone almost as hard as flint, which could be made into axes for chopping down trees and into knives for skinning game. Indeed, so useful was this rock that it became the basis of the first-ever cottage (or perhaps cave) industry of the Lakes, with axeheads exported from Gunmer Crag's axe factory to the rest of Britain.

There are large numbers of oval mounds scattered among the fells where ancient chieftains were buried. They are all high above the valley floors and they help to show where people lived. Unfortunately, at that time nobody gave a thought to the consequences of tree clearance and cultivation on such steep, erodible land. They did not know (as soil scientists now tell us) that nutrients are taken up by plants as they grow, and returned to the soil again when they die. They did not realise that, when this cycle is broken by taking plants away for food, the soil can become infertile for ever. They did, however, discover that, because the soil became useless for crops after a few years, they had continually to clear fresh ground. In this way, by accident rather than by design, the upper forests were slowly cleared. With the nutrients now washed away or used up by the crops, and with domestic animals grazing over the land, oak and ash forests could not regenerate in the abandoned sites and the vegetation changed for ever.

There were still many tribes living up on the fells when the Romans invaded Britain. Considering the trouble the Romans had in subduing mountain peoples elsewhere in Britain, you might have thought they would have left Lakeland well alone. Yet they crossed it with roads and a whole string of forts to guard them. And the reason? The Romans had a sharp eye for metal ore, and Lakeland proved to be a rich source. Besides, despite the difficult terrain, it was easier (or at least quicker) to reach the garrisons in the Vale of Eden between the Lakes and Pennines by taking a direct line across the fells rather than skirting round them. They therefore built some of the most spectacular roads in Britain, including one that runs above 1700 ft (518 m) and gives the fell ridge of High Street near Hayeswater its name. There was a port at Ravenglass, and a fort at Hardknott to guard the pass and others at Ambleside, Kendal and elsewhere. Yet, despite their road network, the Romans probably altered the landscape little – which is more than can be said for the waves of invaders who reached the area on the heels of the Romans as they finally departed from Britain.

When the Romans arrived in Britain, the climate was already getting both colder and wetter. As a result, it was no longer feasible to farm the upland fells and the new Viking invaders and their families began to clear new ground for their crops. Despite the stories about Vikings wanting to do nothing more than to rape and pillage, they were actually a fairly stable people, simply looking out for new land to settle. Theirs was a true folk movement, bringing not just warlords and soldiers, but also the kids, granny and even Great Aunt Brünnhilde, who were all needed to help clear the ground in the densely wooded valleys.

The Vikings were not the only settlers to clear land. Over the centuries the people of Celtic origin (the true British?) had already been forced down into the valleys and off the fells by the deteriorating climate. Although there were probably brief skirmishes as the invaders pushed gradually inland, quite soon they settled down together. After all, there was still plenty of room for everyone and the most important task was to grow sufficient food to keep alive.

You can get a vivid impression of the country of the Celts and the Vikings by looking at the village and fell names on the Ordnance Survey maps. Most of the old Celtic folk were not village dwellers, and they seemed to have no permanent settlements before Viking times. However, this did not deter them from naming the rivers and fells in graphic terms. By contrast, the Vikings were firmly rooted in small hamlets based on clearings hacked out of the valley woodland. These later people named their clearings and their hamlets after the countryside in which they lived. Thus *thwaite* is Viking for 'clearing in a forest', *Rothay* 'a stream full with trout', *Scafell* 'a hill with good upland pasture', and so on.

With such hard work involved in clearing the land, Vikings chose their village sites and farmland with the utmost care. No Viking would have built on fertile soil, nor in a place that might be flooded. At the same time, a supply of water from a spring would be useful, as also would a site near enough to the fell pastures as well as to the valley fields. As a result, settlements were mostly away from flood-prone rivers, on poorer ground way up a fellside, preferably near a spring. In Little Langdale, for example, the buildings of Fell Foot Farm lie in the shelter of a rock-knoll (on the right of our photograph),

(Opposite) **Fell Foot Farm, Little Langdale, seen from 1, Walk 10**

Memory of a once proud culture: the Viking cross at Gosforth

on the main route through Wrynose Pass, and are centred on the scarce lowland fields. The buildings are also on land clear from any floods. Troutbeck (literally 'trout stream') village near Ambleside is strung out along a line of springs away from the fertile valley floor, flooded in winter but providing hay in the summer.

Suitable sites for settlements were hard to come by and, in any case, much of the land was poor, even in the valleys, as the names again testify. Stonethwaite in Borrowdale, for example, has always been a hamlet in a clearing among the stones – exactly as it appears today (Walk 4). Yet, despite the difficulties, these determined and hardy people gave the area its enduring pattern of villages, hamlets and towns.

Little changed after this period for perhaps a thousand years. Somewhere afar a king called Harold was killed and another called William took over and brought with him some armed men to build a few castles out on the plain. Monks occasionally came and went from their monasteries beside the sea (at Furness), but these were only very slight distractions from the main challenge of survival. However, land was progressively cleared and feudal lords and abbots brought large flocks of sheep to graze on the fells, thereby changing the pattern of farming. There were outside influences, too, for Lakeland farmers have always been traders in a small way and their farms simply did not provide all that was needed. Clay pots, for example, had to come from the coast, as also did salt and grain for bread. In exchange, wool and cloth – and, increasingly, metal ore – were provided from the valleys.

Trade involves movement of people, but how did they get about in this difficult country? Clearly, the only way was on foot, by horse (or more likely donkey), and by boat on the lakes. In any case, frequent inclement weather meant it was imperative to use the shortest route possible, just as the Romans had done over a thousand years earlier, even if this did mean a journey across the fells or through a high pass. Even the cattle drovers from Scotland on their way to sell their animals in the markets of Northern England came slowly over the fells because they knew they could get grazing there. With this continual movement, recognised tracks or 'pack-horse roads' came into being.

The routes of pack-horse roads can be spectacular. Their 'engineers' were just as ready to take a route over a fell as through a valley, indeed more so because the valleys were still marshy in many places. The only pack-horse road from Ambleside to Keswick goes straight over Armboth Fell at 1500 ft (457 m), and the Walna Scar road struck out from Coniston up over Seathwaite Fell at more than 1700 ft (518 m) before descending to the Duddon valley. Although they chose the best routes, it was never possible to use them beyond the summer because they became impassable and blocked with snow in winter; yet cattle droves and trains of pack-horses still trampled the ground severely. This was especially serious at stream banks, making crossing ever more difficult. Thus the characteristic stone

(Opposite) **Stockley Bridge (4, Walk 4)**

The early Viking settlers in Lakeland were much more acutely aware of, and constrained by, their surroundings than we are today. Hardly surprising, therefore, that they named their hamlets after the character of the places where they lived. See how appropriate these names are as you follow the walks and drives in this guide. To help you, the origins of some of the most common words are given below. Many names are made of two parts, one part being the description of the area and the other someone's name (e.g. Ravenglass: *raven* the part, *glass* a name; hence Ravenglass means 'the part (of land) belonging to Glas'). At other times both parts are descriptive (e.g. Colwith: *col* of burning wood, *with* forest; thus Colwith means 'a forest where charcoal was burned').

barrow   a hill (e.g. Barrow by Derwentwater)

beck   a stream (e.g. Troutbeck)

brigg   a bridge, stepping-stones (e.g. Brigstone moss, near Elterwater)

by   a homestead (e.g. Soulby, near Dacre)

coom, combe, cove   a hollow in the side of a hill (e.g. Gillercoom, Borrowdale)

dale, den   a valley (e.g. Mickleden, Langdale)

dodd   a hill with a blunt summit that is part of a larger hill (e.g. Skiddaw Dodd)

dore   an opening between walls of rock (e.g. Lodore)

dub   pot-hole in the stream bed (e.g. Swan Dub, Stonethwaite)

ea, ay   water (e.g. Hayeswater: in effect this means water water!)

fell   bare, elevated land (e.g. Armboth Fell)

force   a waterfall (e.g. Skelwith Force)

garth   enclosed ground (e.g. Dalegarth)

gate   a road (not a gate) (e.g. Gatescarth)

gill, ghyll   a gorge with a rapid stream (e.g. Dungeon Ghyll)

grange   a large (feudal) farmhouse and buildings (e.g. Grange, Borrowdale)

hause   a narrow passage like a throat (e.g. Esk Hause)

how   a gentle hill within a vale (e.g. Low How, Grange)

keld   a spring or well (e.g. Threkeld)

knot   a rocky hill (e.g. Hardknott)

mere   a lake (e.g. Buttermere)

nab, ness   a promontory (e.g. Bowness-on-Windermere)

pike, stickle   anything pointed (e.g. Langdale Pikes)

raise   a heap of stones made into a burial chamber (e.g. Dunmail Raise)

rake   a strip of ground that forms a little pass among rocks (e.g. Rakefoot, near Keswick)

rigg   a ridge (e.g. Loughrigg, Ambleside)

scar, scarth, carr   a bare rock outcrop in the form of a cliff (e.g. Gatescarth)

tarn   a small lake high up in the mountains (e.g. Harrop Tarn)

thorpe   a secondary settlement (e.g. Hackthorpe)

thwaite   a clearing in a forest (e.g. Seathwaite)

wath   a ford (e.g. Wath Bridge)

with   a wood, forest (e.g. Colwith)

wyke, wick   an embayment (e.g. Lowick (leafy bay in the hills))

Some others not so easy to sort out:

Blea Tarn   *blue* lake

Dow Crag   *gloomy* rock

*Kes*wick   *cheese* farm

*Kirk*stone   a *church*-like stone

Sty Head   the head of a *stepped path*

bridges came into being. Built across the becks where there was firm rock on both banks, these small simple bridges caused the first in a long series of route realignments that were to culminate with 19th-century valley turnpike roads for coaches and eventually for motor cars. Stockley Bridge was one of many such bridges, its low walls designed to be clear of the horses' packs. Today, fortunately, most of the pack-horse roads remain strictly for the walker.

Ore, slate and railway

A Lake District writer, A. G. Bradley, in his tour of Lakeland just after the First World War, summed up the last phase of Lakeland's pastoral history neatly when he wrote:

> Its story is merely such as can be made by pastoral people, scarcely affected by the outer world or by the usual feudal and social cleavages; neither makers of history, nor builders of castles and abbeys . . . a people who within measurable time have neither been trampled upon, nor trampled upon others; who have merely desired to be let alone, and from their situation have offered small temptation to others to meddle with them.

Perhaps Bradley's ideal example of this tranquil history would be Grasmere village, now beside the main Kendal–Keswick trunk road. This village, its little street packed with holiday-makers all summer long, was, until the 18th century, accessible only by a pack-horse track. No wheels rolled past the village doors, and the bells that now hang in the church tower were dragged in from Ambleside on a sledge.

Although almost complete isolation of this kind did exist, elsewhere there was much pressure to improve communications, especially where mines were in operation. Mining probably started before even the Romans arrived, but the main impact of the search for precious metals stems from the times of the Tudors. Elizabeth the First even went to the trouble of importing specialist German miners to do the work. These, and later miners, scoured the remote fellsides looking for the tell-tale signs of the presence of metals – an ore-rich piece of scree here, an ore-streaked boulder in a stream there – in a sort of Tudor Klondyke fever. The more people looked, the more they found. There was lead and zinc, iron and graphite, copper and silver, for the taking. However, locating the ore seams was one thing, refining out the metal quite another. Thus, quite naturally, the richest and easiest seams were mined first and the others were left. Refining involved separating the metal from the rock by heating in bloomeries, clay hearths in which the ore was laid and then piled high into a cone with charcoal, covered with turf, ignited and then left to burn, perhaps for weeks or even months. The search for ore made some of the first scars on the landscape, in the form of great piles of rock spoil, and further depleted the local forests as wood was cut for charcoal to fuel the voracious bloomeries.

At first, the timber disappeared fast, as trees were felled and not replaced. But gradually, as it became clear that not only was wood

running out but metal-working was here to stay, the trees were felled, not completely but in such a way as to promote new growth from the tree base, a practice called coppicing. Today, many of Lakeland's woods show evidence of coppicing, although they are cut no longer. Many others have been replanted only recently. Thus, few of Lakeland's forests have large, mature trees.

However, it was not only the miners who began to alter the landscape. As demand for building stone (particularly roofing 'slate') from the surrounding lowlands grew, so quarries were opened and some of the fells began to show where man's activities had gnawed deep into their sides.

All this industry began well before, and continued through, the so-called Industrial Revolution of the 18th and 19th centuries. Although many of the worst excesses of industrialisation passed by central Lakeland, the demands for metals saw new mines opened and yet more forest felled (although coke replaced charcoal as a fuel, the coal mines of the Cumberland coast needed timber for pit props). Wood was also in demand for bobbin-making – a Lakeland speciality and Cumbria's main contribution to the Lancashire textile industry. However, the famous linsey-woolsey linen and wool yarn remained little more than a cottage industry: not for Lakeland the dark satanic mills. Only Kendal began to be drawn into the new revolution. In the first years of the 19th century, a canal was cut to connect the town with the Lancashire coalfield and its industries. This was a vital link, enabling Kendal to import coal, ship out slate and ore, and manufacture wool and leather goods. In turn, this trade stimulated the building of newer and better roads, and the era of the stage-coach dawned.

The last major change to affect the Lakeland landscape was also a product of the Industrial Revolution. In the 1850s, the railway gradually stretched out its iron tentacles and encircled the mountains. Although built primarily to serve the industrial towns of the lowlands beyond the Lakes, and to provide access for mines in places such as Eskdale and Coniston, there was an interesting and at first unforeseen spin-off. As industrialisation overtook the British people, so their perception of the landscape began to change. In the 18th century, lowlanders were still afraid of the uplands and mostly avoided them. Even the traveller and poet, Thomas Gray, positively declined to travel as far as the Honister Pass in Borrowdale, having already crept along from Lodore to Rosthwaite in silence lest the crags above should fall and crush him! However, by the 19th century, people were embracing, not cowering away from, their mountain heritage, and the railway took them there. Kendal, and then Keswick, blossomed with a new industry: tourism. Windermere was developed from nothing into a smart holiday resort of considerable size simply because this was the nearest point the railway could come to the lakes. Soon people were flocking into Lakeland to walk, scramble and take the air, and to be transported around the lakes by steamer. Within just a few years, visiting the Lakes was as fashionable as

(Opposite) **The scars of Force Crag mine (right) in the remote fells near Eel Crags (4, Walk 2)**

The countryside today 27

visiting the Alps, and much cheaper. The more wealthy began to build secluded villas possessing views over the lakes and proximity to the railway. The many hotels between Ambleside and Coniston are mostly converted from these spacious and well sited Victorian villas.

Although, by the Second World War, much had been altered within the Lakes, the area still retained a unique charm, having fortunately escaped the ravages of housing-estate development that assailed so many other beauty spots. To protect the landscape, the Lake District National Park was created in 1951, not so much to fossilise a part of England as to ensure that its landscape continued to develop in an orderly and harmonious way for the enjoyment of all. Since then, the Lakeland planning authorities have made some tough decisions in their attempts to conserve the region. They have prohibited the indiscriminate building of holiday homes, the wholesale widening of the little country lanes, the conversion of pastureland into car parks, and so on. If you are sometimes frustrated by the lack of parking space or the narrowness of the roads, perhaps you will agree that such irritations are a small price to pay. Of course, restrictions on driving encourage you to enjoy Lakeland in the best way possible, the way the workers of the Stone Age factories, the Romans and the Vikings saw it – on foot!

ALDER
(65–130 ft; 20–40 m)

A tree of moist lowland and riverside, even the nut-like seeds of the alder are able to float and so be distributed by water. The small, blunt leaves remain green long after those on other trees have fallen. The alder commonly branches from the base to give more than one main stem.

(Opposite) **Immature woodland near the Lodore Cascades (Walk 3)**

Lakeland weather

Planning holidays well in advance involves taking pot-luck with the weather. Nevertheless, day by day, it is possible to choose a walk or a drive that will be pleasant and attractive, even under cloudy and rainy skies. This chapter will help you to understand a little of what causes Lakeland weather, to forecast what might be in store for the day ahead, and to make the most of your stay.

We will start with some differences within Lakeland that occur irrespective of the general weather. Temperatures decrease as you go higher. Thus, on the coast at St Bees, it might be 68°F (20°C) while on Scafell the air temperature will be only 58°F (14°C). As a rule of thumb you can expect temperatures to fall by about 3°F (about 1.8°C) for every 1000 ft (300 m) of ascent. Another change in weather occurs between sheltered and exposed places. In a valley air may be motionless, but you can almost guarantee there will be a breeze on the fellsides and in many cases a fair wind on the tops. A drop in temperature or a strong breeze may bring you out in goose pimples; consequently the combination of cool air and a breeze creates effects far more severe than the simple sum of the two. Scientists refer to the loss of body heat under these circumstances as 'windchill', which in its most severe form is commonly known as 'exposure'. It is common sense to guard against the changes that occur between sheltered valley and exposed fell by taking some woollies with you.

Most of Britain's weather is brought by winds blowing from the Atlantic, so first look westwards (to the sea) for any signs of change. As the air skims over the thousands of miles of ocean between America and Britain, it is hardly surprising that it becomes more and more moist. The amount of moisture that air can hold depends on how warm the air is; because air passing over Lakeland is forced to rise, it cools, thereby reducing its capacity for moisture. The amount to be shed on any one occasion is very hard to predict. If you are lucky, it will be no more than is needed to form small clouds; if you are less lucky, a bit more will condense and the clouds will begin to merge; and if you are really unlucky, the clouds will be unable to hold all the excess moisture and then you will need an umbrella (or, in Lakeland, more sensibly a waterproof nylon coat). It is the unpredictability of the cloud that makes the weather forecaster's job so difficult. In any case, the forecast you hear on the radio is mainly designed for lowland areas and may not be very appropriate for the Lakeland fells. Better, therefore, to phone for the local weather report (dial Windermere 5151) or read the sky for yourself as outlined in the diagrams that follow.

(Opposite) **The heart of Lakeland is its timeless pastoral scenes: the natural livelihood of the farmers must be preserved while catering for the needs of tourists, because without them the landscape would soon be dead**

(a) Uniform, deep, low cloud over the fells is unlikely to clear quickly: avoid routes on the high fells and try either the coast (Walk 14) (where you may find hazy sunshine) or the Vale of Eden and Kendal (where the cloud may have disappeared)

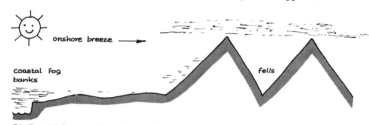

(b) Coastal fog usually only extends inland for a few miles although the moist air it portends may also give cloud on the high fells: try a day between the two, say at Loweswater (Drive 3)

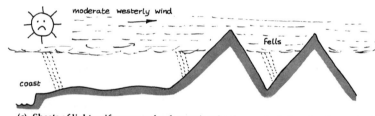

(c) Sheets of light uniform grey cloud, covering the sky evenly, belong to a depression which may not bring rain over the lowland – but rain is more certain over the fells and the cloud is unlikely to disperse: try using the morning for shopping and a leisurely pub lunch followed by a drive (Drive 2) or a coastal walk (Walk 14)

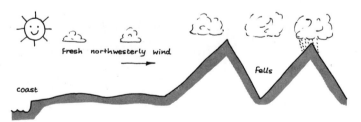

(d) Billowing clouds that start to build from a sparkling clear sky in the early morning may cause overcast sky by midday (this will happen first on the fells) and rain showers are likely in the afternoon but, between the showers, the rain-washed air gives crystal-clear visibility and interesting cloud shadows: this is good weather for photographing landscapes, for a morning walk in the high fells (Walk 4, 5 or 8), or for a drive among them (Drive 1, 2 or 3)

(e) A hot sunny period of settled weather over coast and fell is foretold by the rhyme 'Red sky at night, shepherd's delight', and the red sky is caused by the rays of the setting Sun being bounced off tiny dust particles in the air (dust only accumulates like this under a region of high pressure): good weather for all routes, but a handicap to landscape photographers because there is no cloud and there will almost certainly be haze

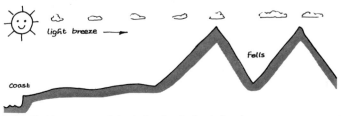

(f) Small white cotton wool clouds that float in the sky but do not grow are a guarantee of fine sunny weather everywhere: visibility will be good and these 'fun clouds' highlight the sky for landscape photography

Have a nice day!

Lakeland climate

There is a considerable difference between climate and daily weather. Climate statistics are assembled from averages over many years and they have very little to do with your holiday weather. However, on average, Seathwaite in Borrowdale does have the unhappy distinction of being the wettest lowland place in England (at 130 in (3300 mm) a year). Similar long-term averages will tell us, by contrast, that the chances of a rainy day in Lakeland are only a little greater than for London: it is mostly that, when rain does fall, there is more of it and it falls harder.

Actually, there are about as many dry days in Lakeland as further south in England, but there are many fewer hours of sunshine because the fells make cloud build up more often. You can expect only half as many hours of sunshine in the fells as on the coast barely 20 miles (32 km) away. But then, no one goes to Lakeland for the sunshine alone, and no mountain scene is really complete without dramatic clouds in the sky. The occasional cloud and the cooler interlude it brings are also welcomed by most walkers and ramblers.

This is the general picture, but within Lakeland there is considerable variation in the weather, especially in relation to the likelihood of rain. The coast and some inland areas of lowland in the lee of Lakeland (such as near Penrith) have less than 40 in (1000 mm) of rain each year. Even some towns surrounded by fells have relatively low rainfall. Both Keswick and Kendal, for example, have less than 60 in

(1520 mm) a year. However, towards central Lakeland, the frequency of cloud and rainfall increases. Grasmere village can expect about 80 in (2030 mm) of rain to fall on its green fields each year and, if you really want to increase your chances of a soaking, try Great End near Sty Head (Route 12), where something like 185 in (4700 mm) of rain and snow fall every year.

Finally, the long-term figures do have something cheery to tell us. The best chances of sunshine and lowest rainfall are in the months of May and June – quiet months anyway, with the leaves still fresh and green on the trees. If you cannot manage an early holiday, try an Autumn break around late September and October, for these are also relatively dry months with the added bonus of the trees in their full Autumn russet glory.

A word about the fells

At the time Black's *Picturesque guide to the English Lakes* was written in 1866, tourism was in its infancy, signposts unknown, the land largely unmapped, and tracks unworn. As a result visitors were in some difficulty without the help of local people. With this in mind the following sound advice was offered:

> Guides can be procured at any of the neighbouring inns, who, for a moderate compensation, will conduct strangers to the summit(s) by the least circuitous path(s). . . . Fine clear days should be selected for an expedition of this kind, as well for the advantage of having extensive prospect, as for safety. Mists and wreaths of vapour, capping the summits of mountains, or creeping along their sides, are beautiful objects when viewed from the lowly valley; but when the wanderer becomes surrounded with them on the hills they occasion anything but agreeable sensations and have not in-frequently led to serious accidents.

Although guides are a feature of the past, the rest is sound advice for, even with footpaths sometimes worn as broad as motorways, and with fine maps and a compass, the fells in the mist are still best left to their own solitude.

KINGFISHER

Near to many streams the sapphire-blue splash of colour that flashes from one bank to another may be your first glimpse of a kingfisher. It is an extremely shy bird, but look out for it sitting on a branch overhanging the water. It uses the branch as a diving board to help it catch small fish. Kingfishers nest in tunnels dug deep into river banks.

PART 2   ROUTES

Views: getting your bearings

If you pick up a map of Lakeland, or look at the many public foot-path signs beside the roads, or skim through the pages of this book, you will see a bewildering number of names describing every last mountain and hill. From the centre of the region, with mountains on all sides, the pattern of fells is especially difficult to grasp. It is far better not to make for the centre of Lakeland but to pause near the outskirts, where you can begin to appreciate the Lakeland scene from the nearby hills. The three walks that follow will help you to begin to put the landscape into perspective. The first is but a few steps from a car park near Kendal, the second an easy 20-minute walk from the centre of Windermere, and the third from a hill overlooking Keswick.

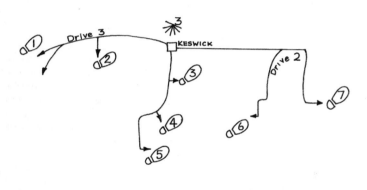

Routes from
Keswick and
Ambleside

1　From Kendal: Scout Scar

Introduction

➤ Take road opposite Kendal Town Hall (and information centre) [Scout Scar >]

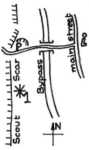

How to get to Scout Scar from Kendal

If you come to Lakeland from the south, the first town beyond the motorway is Kendal. Famous the world over for its mint-cake sweets, it is a thriving shopping, touring and entertainment centre, and, despite its popularity, Kendal has managed to retain much of its charm.

Kendal's whole history is linked with the routeway gap in the limestone hills through which the River Kent flows. The strategic site of the town has been recognised and jealously guarded for over a thousand years. From the remains of the castle you can enjoy a low-level view over the town, but a far more sweeping panorama is seen from the top of the limestone itself – on Scout Scar, only a couple of miles away.

The view

🅿 in quarry on ridge crest

🐚 Cross road, walk up grassy slope, then along ridge to mushroom; ✷ sketched diorama on inside rim

From the moment you leave the car in the quarry, the local view is dominated by large cliffs of dove-grey limestone. Here the limestone appears to have been formed into horizontal beds, its great blocks making near-vertical natural stone walls. It is the ability of the limestone to withstand the effects of erosion that has allowed it to form the imposing ridge of Scout Scar.

Although not the most attractive structure ever made by man, the mushroom viewpoint is an excellent place for a spectacular view northwards to the central fells, southwards to the Irish Sea and eastwards to the Pennines. The highest rocks in view are also the oldest. Standing boldly against the sky and directly across from Scout Scar are the masses of Dow Crag and the Old Man of Coniston (2631 ft; 802 m). These form the southernmost salient of the tough volcanic rocks of the central fells. Between them and the mushroom lie the younger, mudstone rocks that cradle Coniston Water and Windermere, although both lakes remain hidden from view. To the left of Dow Crag are the granite fells that stretch southwards towards Morecambe Bay, reaching near to the sea at Ravenglass. Then, left again, is the shimmering water of Morecambe Bay itself.

Swinging northwards from the Old Man of Coniston lie the grander fells. The highest peak, just right of the Old Man, is Scafell (3206 ft; 977 m); then, right again, lies Bowfell (2960 ft; 902 m) and the steep-sided peaks that lie beside Langdale, of which the highest is Harrison Stickle (2403 ft; 732 m). Then the fells become slightly lower before the broad mass of Helvellyn (3116 ft; 950 m) dominates the northern skyline.

Look directly north, parallel to the edge of Scout Scar. Here you will find the easternmost of the volcanic fells culminating in High Street (2719 ft; 829 m). Beside them to the right lie the further granite hills of the Shap Fells, which have a characteristically knobbly form. To the east of the Shap Fells is the major gap of the Eden valley – the lowland corridor between Lakeland and the Pennines through which the M6 runs. Then, immediately east, are the Yorkshire Dales – the part of the Pennines dominated by the tableland hills of Whernside (left) and Ingleborough (right).

Spend a little while looking around with the help of a map. A short walk across the crest of Scout Scar eastwards will soon bring Kendal into view, its strategic gap position very clearly visible. Similarly, an even shorter walk from the mushroom towards the scar edge (take care: the edge is vertical) will give you a superb view of part of the girdle of limestone that surrounds Lakeland.

Although, in the quarry, the limestone looks as though its 'bricks' were formed into horizontal courses, they are really leaning very slightly to the south-east. This becomes clearer from the scar top. Now eroded back to the edges of the Lake District, these limestones once swept like a majestic canopy over all the rocks to the north; the boulder-covered slopes below the scar show that erosion is still continuing. Every winter, rain enters the cracks in the exposed scar. The rain water freezes and expands, gradually pitching yet more blocks to the slope below. Indeed, the whole of the scar top is littered with the same frost-shattered debris – loose flakes of limestone that crackle underfoot like broken glass.

Return to **P** via scar edge

The walk from the mushroom back to the quarry car park along the edge of the scar gives not only a splendid view and an opportunity to see the work of the weather in eroding the landscape, but also an idea of the scale of the forces deep within the Earth that have crushed and lifted all the rocks of Lakeland. Look along the scar northwards and you will find that it is discontinuous. The section north of the road is set back and at a slightly different orientation from the scar. Between the two lies a small broken fragment of the scar angled awkwardly like a badly set fractured bone. In the distant past, this huge mass of limestone has been broken apart (faulted) by huge subsurface forces. Agents of the weather have been quick to use these natural points of weakness, creating a lower gap in the scar edge. Man has also taken advantage of the same feature to provide an easy route into Kendal from Windermere lake. In the long turbulent history of Lakeland this is only a small feature. Far more spectacular earth movements occurred to the north, as will be seen from both Orrest Head and Latrigg (Views 2 and 3).

2   From Windermere: Orrest Head

town centre

How to get to Orrest Head from Windermere

🏃 [Orrest Head >] opposite railway station and **ℹ**

Introduction

While Kendal thrived on the age-old trade between upland and lowland, the site that was to be Windermere town remained pastureland, the home of just a few farmers. It was not natural advantages that formed Windermere town, but the single most important force of the 19th century – the railway. It seems almost as though, after heaving and puffing over the Lakeland foothills beyond Kendal, the railway took one look at the mountains ahead and decided to go no further. Windermere town grew up as a railway terminus and is now a jumping-off place for further adventures deep within the fells. It is near to Lakeland's longest lake (Windermere; 10½ miles; 17 km) and within sight of the highest fells. Orrest Head is a mere 758 ft (231 m) high and rises less than 600 ft (183 m) above lake level, but it gives a view comparable to that from fells three times its height.

The view

As you walk along the winding road between screens of rhododendron bushes, you soon find evidence that the area has been more disturbed than Scout Scar at Kendal. Occasionally a small piece of bare rock is left exposed, or the face of an old quarry appears amid the trees. Each of these modest exposures of stone tells a story of great upheaval in the past, since every bed of rock thrusts vertically from the ground rather than lying horizontally in the manner in which it was first laid down.

The flanks of the hill are mantled with the

✳ A diorama board
stands near the seats

boulder clay left behind after the Ice Age. This thins
rapidly towards the summit, and the top is of bare,
ice-gouged, limy mudstone. Here, above the level
of the nearby trees, is one of the loveliest views
from the lowland lakes: below, spreading away to
the south, lie the glistening waters of Windermere.
Despite its great size, Windermere lake was not
gouged out very deeply by ice and was even partly
refilled by glacial debris as the Ice Age waned.
Indeed, if it had not been for a great ridge of
debris blocking the southern end of the valley and
impounding the lake, there would probably be no
more than a few, tiny, isolated sheets of water.

Each of the many islands off shore from Bowness
is a high mound of boulder clay. Had the lake level
been fractionally lower, the islands might well have
united to split the lake in two.

Directly down the lake and over Windermere
town you look southwards towards Morecambe
Bay and the Irish Sea. From this direction scan
the landscape clockwise over the relatively low,
granite Ulpha fells of Eskdale, on to the nearer and
much higher outlines of Dow Crag and the Old
Man of Coniston (2631 ft; 802 m). Although they
appear as a distant rise on the northwestern skyline
when viewed from Scout Scar, their shap take on
more detail from Orrest Head. Lying direcutly westwards Dow Crag and the Old Man are now only
7 miles (11 km) away beyond the hidden lake of
Coniston Water. These are the southernmost out-
posts of the central fells, the tough volcanic rocks
that make the bold, craggy outlines of Lakeland's
highest peaks. Immediately to the right of the Old
Man and set back a little is Crinkle Crags (2816 ft;
858 m). Half hidden behind it is the highest peak in
Lakeland – Scafell Pike (3206 ft; 977 m). Next,
follows the broader back of Bowfell (2960 ft; 902 m)
at the head of Borrowdale, then the Langdale Pikes
dominated by Harrison Stickle at 2403 ft (732 m).

The Langdale Pikes lie almost in a direct line with
the shorter, northerly arm of Windermere. In front
of them, and less than 5 miles (8 km) away, lies the
lower fell of Loughrigg (1099 ft; 335 m) beside the
town of Ambleside. To the right again, and virtually due north, rears the broad back of Helvellyn
(3113 ft; 949 m) with Dollywagon Pike (2810 ft;
856 m) immediately in front of it and Fairfield
(2863 ft; 873 m) keeping close company to the
right. All these peaks guard the western shores of
Ullswater whose eastern end is delineated by the
slightly lower mass of High Street (2719 ft; 829 m).

Views 42

Slightly to the east of north, the knobbly Shap Fells come into view. These granite fells mark the edge of central Lakeland and soon fall away to the Vale of Eden. The last line of hills is much more distant and is formed in the massive limestones of the Pennines. Some 30 miles (48 km) away, the flat-topped peaks of Whernside and Ingleborough are rarely more than shadowy silhouettes on the eastern skyline, but they serve to illustrate Lakeland's isolation from the rest of upland Britain.

With this brief overview of the peaks complete, you can better appreciate the great dome-like form of the central fells, even though this has been partly removed by millions of years of erosion by water and ice.

3   From Keswick: Latrigg

Introduction

How to get to Latrigg from Keswick

⬧ 🅿 opposite bungalows and follow wide gravel track [Skiddaw >]

Many would say that Lakeland's most spectacular scenery lies towards the north, and certainly Keswick has the most imposing setting of all the Lakeland towns. With a backdrop formed by the massive domes of Skiddaw (3054 ft; 931 m) and Blencathra (2841 ft; 866 m), and views directly down Derwentwater towards the central fells, its position is hard to rival. However, the ring of high fells makes the lowland views less extensive than those from Windermere and Kendal. For this reason a good view can only be obtained from higher ground, for example from Latrigg, a hill that rises just north of the town. Isolated from the main mass of Skiddaw, it offers spectacular views along valleys stretching for tens of miles.

The view

The path to Latrigg runs over very different rocks from those of either Scout Scar or Orrest Head. Everywhere lie small, dark grey flakes of shale, the frost-shattered remnants of an ancient ocean mud. These rocks have succumbed relatively easily to the ravages of the weather so that Latrigg, like its nearby giant neighbours of Skiddaw and Blencathra, has a smoother, rounded form. Its sweeping slopes contrast markedly with the broken rugged grandeur of the more distant mountains standing starkly against the southern skyline.

The view from Latrigg (1203 ft; 367 m) shows not only the majesty of the Lakeland landscape but also a bird's-eye view of the way man has tried to get to grips with nature and adapt it for his own benefit. The highlight of the view is the broad, shimmering lake of Derwentwater set amid the highest of the fells. Dominating all the fells is the rounded summit of Great Gable (2949 ft; 899 m), a full 10 miles (16 km) distant. This is a vista of the tough volcanic Central Fell rocks at their most impressive. Great Gable is surrounded by other, slightly less prominent, fells, such as the narrow dinosaur-like ridge whose backbone humps undulate up to High Spy (2143 ft; 653 m) and culminate in Dale Head (2473 ft; 754 m). To their right, and separated by the wide, open Newlands valley, lies the mass of Eel Crag and Crag Hill (2753 ft; 839 m), with the isolated peak of Causey Pike on one of its buttress ridges. Causey Pike is particularly interesting because it separates the rugged central fells of volcanic rocks from the nearer, lower and more rounded slate fells, such as its lakeside neighbour, Cat Bells (1481 ft; 451 m).

From Latrigg you can look out slightly to the right (west) of Derwentwater down on to the village of Braithwaite, tucked in beneath the forested slopes of the rounded fells sliced by the Whinlatter Pass. All these fells are of slates and their summits rarely rise to 2000 ft (610 m).

To the left (east) of Great Gable lies more volcanic rock scenery, rising to Glaramara (2560 ft; 780 m) and (behind it) Bowfell (2960 ft; 902 m) at the head of Langdale. Further left, the distant view is obscured by the nearby broad fell of Castlerigg (1932 ft; 589 m). Beyond this lies Thirlmere reservoir, tucked out of sight within a deep glacially scoured valley, but there is no mistaking the far side of the lake, for there rises the stark outline of Helvellyn (3116 ft; 950 m) and the ridge that leads northwards to Great Dodd (2807 ft; 856 m).

Now that you have seen one of Britain's finest mountain panoramas, look behind to the Skiddaw and Blencathra fells, their separation from, and contrast with, the central fells made all the more striking by the broad glaciated valley in which Keswick lies.

Imagine the scene some 14 000 years ago when Lakeland was in the grip of the Ice Age. The broad valley that today carries the A66 from Penrith to Workington is filled with ice whose crevassed surface carries huge piles of frost-broken rock from the nearby fells, its underbelly scraping away at the rock and carving the basin that one day will contain Derwentwater. In front of you two ice streams converge, combining their powers to enlarge and deepen the valley leading northwards to the Irish Sea.

The same area some 4000 years on looks dramatically different. The ice has gone and in its place are wide, open valleys, once more developing soils and becoming forested. In the rock-gouged valley floors, a vast lake stretches from the foot of Great Gable along Borrowdale and out along the entire length of Bassenthwaite, where it is held up by piles of ice-dumped debris. Already at this time the lake basins are being infilled as streams cascade down valley sides, carrying debris with them. The first signs of the separation of Derwentwater and Bassenthwaite are here already, as deltas built out from both lake shores.

Finally, the scene a mere 1000 years ago can be imagined as the Vikings saw it when they chose to settle at Keswick. The landscape by now is green and fully clothed with forest, the wide piece of land between Derwentwater and Bassenthwaite a potentially lush water-meadow requiring little forest clearing, and the site of Keswick a good route centre for further exploration inland and towards the central fells. This is virtually the modern scene, when much of the forest has been cleared and the lowland farmed. Until recently, a railway came over the pass from Penrith, and the main roads still do. It looks as though the Vikings chose a good spot for settlement in a land made easier for survival with a little help from Nature.

FLY AGARIC

There is no mistaking this striking toadstool, with its scarlet red cap which has warty white scales. It adds a vivid splash of colour to birch and pine forest floors from late summer to late autumn. Its red colour really does mean danger – it is highly poisonous.

Drives in and around Lakeland

1   The southern fells

Introduction

➮ Begin at
Ambleside on A591

In the southern fells, variety is the keynote. The
grandeur of deep valleys gives way to the high
Lakeland passes, then shimmering lakes and
finally wide, lakeside views. This route includes
the famous Hardknott Pass, with its testing hairpin
bends: there is an alternative route for those who
want a more relaxing drive. Here also are some of
the prettiest valleys in Lakeland: the Esk valley
with its famous railway, and the higher Duddon
valley with its gorges and waterfalls.

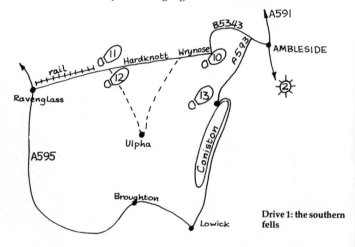

Drive 1: the southern fells

The route

Ambleside ⬛ M WC
∅ ⬛ 🅿 🅿🅾 ⬛

Ambleside lies at the heart of the Lake District:
a true crossroads in the mountains. Here the
main north–south Lakeland artery is met by the
road from Langdale and Coniston and that from
Kirkstone. Yet this pleasant, stone-built town was
scarcely more than an overgrown village before
holiday-makers came to Lakeland. It is a true
fellside town, its main street keeping high above
the marshy land where the River Rothay flows.

(Opposite) **A patch of sunlight highlights the open U-shaped Oxendale (left) and
Mickleden valleys at the head of Great Langdale – notice how the cultivated land is
limited to the valley bottoms: left, Crinkle Crags; centre, Bowfell; right, Langdale Pikes;
the notch on the skyline to the right of Bowfell (Rossett Ghyll) shows where a line of
shattered rocks has been etched out by erosion**

When the woollen industry came to Ambleside, it was the steep course of the Stock Gill, now just a pleasant stream that tumbles below the main street, that provided the water power used by machines to tease out and spin the wool. In fact, if you walk up the hill towards the Kirkstone Pass, you will pass houses with upper windows that tell of the days when the buildings were tiny factories on whose upper floors the weaving was done.

On A593 [Coniston >] (at junction with A5075 (bridge over river), Roman Fort, Galvana, NT �)

The Stock Gill tumbles down to flow into the quieter waters of the River Rothay. Between them the Rivers Rothay and Brathay (which flows into Lake Windermere from the west) are gradually silting up this largest of England's lakes. Today, Windermere is still 10½ miles (17 km) long, but in the distant past it stretched well to the north and west of Ambleside. The Romans, who built a fort on the lake shore, saw a different scene. Today, the fort is more than 100 yds (90 m) back from the shore!

After a brief excursion on to the valley floor, the road from Ambleside to Skelwith Bridge keeps well above the flood-prone River Brathay, which here flows sluggishly over the silts of an old lake bed. This is a sheltered area but with excellent views to the distant fells, and it proved particularly attractive to wealthy Victorians. Today, many of the villas that were once family homes for the summer season have been converted into hotels hidden discreetly behind borders of exotic trees. Although these woodlands are at their colourful best in autumn, when every leaf seems to be of burnished copper or gold, they also provide a leafy glade in summer when only dappled light reaches the road.

At Skelwith Bridge [Great Langdale B5343 >], Elterwater on left (Walk 9)

Elterwater village 🅿 ∅ 🍽 🏧 PO WC

From Elterwater to the head of Great Langdale the fell scenery changes dramatically. In this area glaciers have gouged a deep and wide trough that leaves tributary valleys hanging high above, their waters cascading hundreds of feet down the rocky valley side. Here, too, glaciers dug deep into those rocks of the valley floors that offered least resistance, but were held up by the tougher rocks. As a result the valley floor has become a series of steps, each 'riser' a tough rock bar marked by rapids or a small waterfall (at Clappergate, Skelwith, Elterwater and Thrang bridges) and behind it a 'tread' gouged into a number of deeply worn but now silted-up rock basins. Each of these basins formerly contained a lake, but few remnants now remain. Elterwater is the only sizeable lake and even this is silting up fast.

The old lake floors of the valley steps are often

flooded when their tiny streams cannot cope with the mountain deluges. It is not surprising, therefore, that roads were built to avoid the valley floor, despite having to take a more tortuous valley-side route. Even the farmers, to whom flat land is a precious resource, are limited by the wet land, for trampling by livestock rapidly turns the water-meadows into a quagmire. As a result you will rarely see an animal here, except in the driest times of summer. The main use of these fields is for growing hay.

Dungeon Ghyll Force (waterfall) is behind the New Dungeon Ghyll Hotel 🅿 🍴

Beyond the New Dungeon Ghyll Hotel the road seems to climb straight up the mountain of Bowfell lying directly ahead. On the right, the great bulk of the Langdale Pikes completely bars the way, at least to modern travel. However, not only did Stone Age man use rock from these high fells to make the famous Langdale axes, but he also crossed the fells with 'roadways'. Such routes were in use continuously until the days of the motor car. For instance, the pack-horse road connecting Langdale and Borrowdale goes ahead where your road turns sharp left, following the valley at the head of Langdale and up through the Stake Pass at over 1600 ft (488 m).

Great Langdale and Little Langdale are fortuitously linked by a saddle-shaped pass that takes the road high up on to the fells. It is worth parking at the summit for the superb views. The saddle is not here simply by chance: it has been carved in a continuation of the long belt of shattered and weak rocks stretching from beside Great Gable in the west, down through the valley of Mickleden, across where you now stand, and behind you to the strip of forest on the left above Blea Tarn, where a small stream continues to exploit the weakness.

Walk 11
At junction: right
[Wrynose Pass >]

Blea Tarn, the shimmering pool of water in its glaciated hollow, introduces the Little Langdale valley, whose path follows yet another line of weak and shattered rock. The road along Little Langdale, through the glacially breached divide of Wrynose Pass, across the broad trough of Wrynose Bottom, up into the further glacial breach of Hardknott Pass and down into Upper Eskdale, has a remarkably straight alignment (except for its hairpin bends!) and follows the belt of shattered rock for several miles through otherwise inaccessible country.

As you crest Wrynose Pass (a corruption of the Viking words for Stallion's Pass) there is a superb view back over Little Langdale, its glaciated valley a classic U shape. Ahead are the equally dramatic

The southern fells 51

sights of Wrynose Bottom and the further saddle of Hardknott Pass. Here, too, is the famous Three-shire Stone, marking the old junction of Westmorland, Cumberland and Lancashire. From Wrynose Pass you descend briefly into the valley of the River Duddon whose waters drain directly to the Irish Sea near Ravenglass. This is not, however, just an area where rivers divide. It is also a region from which glaciers probably diverged, spilling from the high fells over lower crests and into the surrounding valleys. Today, Wrynose Bottom carries a diminished River Duddon (here called Eller Dubs) in a confused pattern of meanders. The stream splits over the flat floor of a glaciated valley now littered with boulders, which once scraped away the fellside rocks. It is a wild and barren land, a place where even the vegetation cowers from the cold winter, which lasts much longer here than in the lower Lakeland valleys. Not surprisingly, the old farmhouse on the far bank now lies deserted.

Gatescarth Farm ruins (GR 248020)

Cockley Beck bridge: left [Duddon valley >] *or* right [Hardknott >]. N.B. Hardknott is steep (1 in 3) and with hairpin bends and becomes very congested in high summer

This is a good place to pause to consider whether to tackle the Hardknott Pass or take the easier but longer route to the Duddon valley.

Hardknott Pass. If you think you are having trouble over Hardknott's rough and craggy landscape, spare a thought for the Romans for whom this was the main road from Ambleside, or for the medieval cattle drovers coaxing their animals across mile after mile of windswept peaty wilderness. Even 50 years ago, the Hardknott and Wrynose passes had only a rough track cut across by streams. In the Second World War it was this rough country that appealed to the army as a rigorous testing area for heavy vehicles, but they damaged the track so badly that it had to be completely rebuilt and it was not until this late stage that it became properly surfaced. Today's road runs along a somewhat different route from the old drove and pack-horse road, in the main choosing the opposite side of the valley on its route southwards from Hardknott. The old route passes over Doctor Bridge (now on a side road). After your drive you may care to consider whether the old or the new follows the better route!

M (Roman fort) on right

About half-way down from the pass, the Roman signal station and fort (Mediobogdum) stands proudly on a conspicuous ledge of rock to the right. This superb defensive site uses the last part of the volcanic rocks that have been so important in forming the character of the high fells. It also provides

The entrance to Hardknott Pass, illustrating some of the problems of travel in glaciated uplands

splendid views for holiday-makers. To the north you can trace the glacially scoured Esk valley to its source below Scafell Pike (3206 ft; 977 m). To the west, the whole of the lower Esk valley is laid out almost like a map, its small fields and their stone walls a patchwork of all shades of green on the flat areas near the stream in contrast to the yellow and olive-coloured fellsides. Beyond can be seen the open expanse of the Irish Sea and the blue, misty form of the Isle of Man.

Below the fort the land falls away rapidly as the fells become more subdued. This is granite country and, as on Dartmoor, it is a rich source of minerals. The minerals here are mostly iron, the deposits of which were thick and rich enough to make worthwhile the building of the Eskdale railway. The single line climbs to just below the main mine at Boot, where the Hardknott route rejoins the Duddon valley loop.

Walk 12 Walk 13
Classic Rail 🚂
Boot 🍺

The Duddon valley. Although this diversion traces two sides of a triangle, the route is far easier on the driver, especially in high summer. The glaciers also found Hardknott Pass a difficult route and they, too, mostly flowed SSW to widen the valley

Follow [Ulpha >]

in which the River Duddon now meanders. The drive over Hardknott soon brings you into a quite different, granite-formed landscape, but the Duddon valley is cut into the same volcanic rocks as those forming the central fells. As a result, steep fell slopes rise on either side: to the right Harter Fell, and to the left the great ridge of rock forming the Old Man of Coniston.

As in Langdale, differences in rock resistance have played a great part in shaping the valley floor and have influenced the road gradients. Whenever you change gear to cope with a steeper rock section, look around to see whether, nearby on the fells, there are prominent crags; whether, in the valley below, the River Duddon begins to cascade or flow in a rock-cut gorge; or whether the valley itself suddenly narrows – all signs that you have arrived at a tougher band of rock. The first of these occurs at Birk Bridge, a pretty pack-horse bridge giving you a good view of the river cascading over large boulders. Below Birk Bridge the valley flattens again (the staircase tread) before going into a narrow gorge (the staircase riser) out of sight near Seathwaite and so on.

Seathwaite stands guard at the head of the agricultural Duddon valley. This is a contrast to the land that you have just driven through, which offers farmers little scope. Seathwaite is also important because it stood at the end of the Walna Scar pack-horse road that once carried trade to and from Coniston in the east. Look left from Seathwaite to the fellside and you will see the great 'bite' out of the skyline through which the road passes. Although Seathwaite is a stop on the fell road that continued over to Eskdale and the coast, it is really Ulpha (pronounced 'Oofa') that signifies a return to lower land. Yet Ulpha is more than a strung-out farming village, for in its time it has seen copper mining and the roasting of limestone to produce the lime so vital to agriculture in the predominantly acid soils of the fells. Today, by contrast, it provides a pleasant stop to rest awhile before going on to Eskdale.

The route over Birker Fell between Dunnerdale and Eskdale passes through yet another glacially breached gap in the fells, which have now changed from the harsh crags of the central fells to rather softer, more rounded, forms. From the summit of this road there is a splendid viewpoint looking over the Esk valley and the route to Hardknott Pass. Here, too, you leave the ancient volcanic rocks and

Birk Bridge lies just beyond where the road is joined by a track on right. ⓟ here and walk

Seathwaite ⓔ

Ulpha ⓔ: right [Eskdale >]

400 yds (366 m) left [Devoke Water >]

move on to granite. The junction between the two rocks runs through nearby Devoke Water, a pretty lake set high in a fellside hollow, and the footpath to it runs virtually along the junction. Ahead, the fells beyond the Esk are in granite and there is again an obvious contrast with the harsh fells to the north-east. Can you see the contrast along the footpath?

Combined route (continued)

At end of road T-junction: turn left for Walks 12, 13, Roman fort; turn left to continue drive

The little road that runs beside the lower Esk reveals a completely new landscape as it avoids the flat marshy land of the Esk valley and winds and twists between granite knolls that show many signs of glacial scouring. Rock outcrops are scarce here and most of these knolls have been used as building-stone quarries for farms, although rounded boulders cleared from the fields have also been used. This low, granite country is quickly passed and soon the wide estuary of the Esk appears, now filled with silt eroded from the fells. The valley floor does not rest on rock: that is buried 200 ft (60 m) below!

At A595 turn left

After the high fells you may find the valley less exhilarating, but it makes for much easier driving. From here, you can get a good perspective on the fells as they rise from an almost flat coastal platform 50 ft (15 m) above sea level. Here the road runs on the remains of an ancient beach cut at a time when the sea was higher than it is today.

[Broughton A595 >], then A5092 [Ulverston >]. At Lowick Green turn left onto A5084 [Coniston >]

The return route beside the eastern shores of Coniston Water contrasts with the earlier part of the drive. Here, you are in the valley bottom, the wide glaciated valley in which Coniston Water lies, giving you space to see the Old Man and other fells on the far bank. The contrast between the east and west shores of the lake becomes very clear, for on the far side are the volcanic rocks of the Old Man, whereas beside you are the rounded and subdued slate rocks, which are far less tough. There is also a fine view along the entire length of the lake from its northern end – a final reminder that the whole landscape you have seen is only there because of the Ice Age.

At Lowick Bridge turn left over bridge then left. Road follows Coniston Water

[Coniston >]
[Ambleside >]

2 The northeastern fells

Introduction

This drive, using mostly major roads, skirts around one of England's most famous mountains – Helvellyn. Without stopping, it would take less than 2 hours, but there is so much to see that most of the day may well be needed. Nevertheless, this is the quickest of the three leisure drives and it could occupy a wet afternoon, although, of course, the scenic beauty is seen at its best on a clear sunny day.

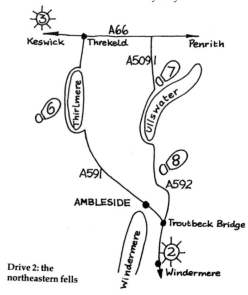

Drive 2: the
northeastern fells

The route

⚓ Begin at Ambleside

In the days before the Normans conquered England, the north-west was still a Viking stronghold. Here the Vikings eked out a living among the harsh fells. The Lakeland scenery must have made these Norwegian folk feel at home, and at Ambleside they found pastureland beside the sluggish waters of the River Rothay as it split and divided over the flat valley floor. The name of their settlement, Ambleside, means 'the farm on a sandbank in the river'. At an early stage the riverside site was abandoned in favour of a drier, hillside position safe from the winter floods, but it took a long time for Ambleside to grow to its present size.

Ambleside 🅿 M WC
🍴 📷 🏛 🎫 ♿ ∅

Industry bypassed Ambleside, although for many years wooden bobbins were made and woollen cloth woven. Its present size is almost entirely a product of the tourist trade for, although the town was located where the north–south

Drives 56

Kendal-to-Keswick track crossed the south-west–north-east Ravenglass-to-Penrith track, the difficult terrain had always hampered trading. After serviceable roads had been built, however, the holiday-makers found that Ambleside was the key to the central fells, as is abundantly clear today from congested streets and crowded pavements.

Leave on A591 south [Windermere >]. In 2 miles (3.2 km) turn left (after Low Wood Hotel) [Troutbeck >]

Ambleside lies on the border of the mountains, which are here made from weak 'slates' whose character is much the same as the slates that give the northern fells their gentler, rounded forms, unlike the tough rocks of the craggy central fells. Yet even though this less rugged fell landscape with its wider valleys is more easily farmed than most of Lakeland, the fields can still only be used for pasture because of a combination of high rainfall (Ambleside can expect 75 in (1900 mm) of rain a year), and heavy clay soils that drain very slowly.

The Troutbeck empties into the deep, still waters of Windermere, dumping its load of silt into the lake. With no current to move the silt it rapidly builds new land, forming a miniature Nile delta. This is valuable flat land – a scarce resource in a region of steep slopes – and it is not to be found again in the valley of the Troutbeck for some miles.

Troutbeck village ⌖

It is possibly better to see Troutbeck village on foot than by car. However, if you drive slowly, you cannot fail to notice how it is strung out across the hill slope, keeping off the good pasture of the valley bottom. Troutbeck is a good mile long but contains no more than a few dozen houses.

The Troutbeck valley, like most of the valleys in Lakeland, really owes its present shape to the scouring effect of glaciers in the Ice Age. It is basically a wide, open U shape, although there is considerable variation in width depending on where the tough and resistant rocks occur. One such rock bar causes the valley to narrow below the village, whereas up stream it is wide and flat. For more than a mile the valley gains no more than 40 ft (12 m) in height. From the road you can see it quite clearly. As you look, try to imagine it covered with water, for this part of the valley was once a lake. The Troutbeck may have made only minor inroads on the shoreline of Windermere, but it soon infilled this little shallow lake, erasing it from the landscape.

Join A592, turn left [Patterdale >]

As you climb steadily along the main road, the soft 'slates' that have flanked the valley to this point are replaced by tough, hard, volcanic rocks. With this change, the more gentle, rounded fells are succeeded by gaunt, rugged peaks with far steeper slopes. The change is quite sudden and equally dramatic. Ahead the Troutbeck narrows and its course steepens until suddenly you see the upper valley now 'hanging' high above the broad lower valley, a change that is largely the result of the presence of tougher rocks near the valley head.

Kirkstone Pass 🅿 🍴 The road leaves the Troutbeck valley and follows the ridge, heading for the famous Kirkstone Pass. A stone resembling the shape of a church (Kirk) has lent its name to this impressive gap in the fells, long since breached by glaciers forcing up from Ullswater towards you.

The road you have followed from Troutbeck may look as though it has been there for ever. However, as in other Lakeland valleys, the modern road differs from that once followed by pack-horses, then by carriages and the post coach. The former, direct Kirkstone Pass road is the minor road that descends to Ambleside opposite the Inn, but is now largely ignored in favour of a more direct route to the rail-head at Windermere. The earlier route is interesting because it uses a conspicuous, level ledge on the fellside, thereby keeping the steep section as short as possible.

Road engineers today prefer long and even gradients, as the new road demonstrates. Nevertheless, despite the change of route, the early road builders clearly made sure they kept the Inn on the main road. It was probably needed, too, because a team of horses pulling up the steep gradient from Ambleside would surely need to be changed by the time they crested the pass.

There are two good viewpoints at Kirkstone. One, opposite the Inn, looks back down the pass to Ambleside; the other, a few hundred yards further on, looks forward to the small pool of Brothers Water.

The next section of the drive contains the most dramatic of all the fells. Yet how could such grand peaks have been given names such as Fairfield (on your left in the Pass) and Dollywagon Pike (next left), which, from the name alone, could as easily be in Surrey as in Lakeland. Perhaps the Viking (Farald) who first owned the high fell (Viking = *fjeld*) after which Fairfield is named is still turning in his grave.

The valley ahead is one enormous ice-scoured trough, rapidly filling with sediment. From the base of Kirkstone Pass beyond Brothers Water to the shores of Ullswater – over 3 miles (5 km) – the valley floor falls hardly at all. Once, Ullswater would have stretched to the base of Kirkstone, but now, after much filling by streams bringing sediment from the mountainsides, only Little Brothers Water is left as a reminder of the size of this former reach of the valley lake.

From Brothers Water it is worth looking back to the pass and the fells that crowd around. These are the mountains that nurtured the early glaciers flowing down to gouge out the Ullswater trench.

Walk 9 However, the glaciers did not work alone. On the left of the pass they must have been joined by glaciers from the valley that now contains Hayeswater. Yet dominating all of these glaciers, ice poured from the deep sheltered hollows overlooking Ullswater on its western side, for these are the great combes and coves of the Helvellyn range. Like great icy tongues these glaciers must have converged on Ullswater making it even deeper. Individually, each glacier could accomplish only a limited scouring, but when combined their effect was far greater. As a result, the tributary glaciers were left progressively 'higher and drier' as the ice stream they supplied cut even deeper.

Both the main valley of Ullswater and the tributary hanging valleys such as Grisedale run south-west to north-east following the 'grain' of the ancient volcanic rocks into which they have been cut. From time to time, however, the grain has been cut across, more or less at right angles, giving to the Ullswater valley a distinctive dog-leg appearance.

Grisedale House Pass, 2004 ft (611 m) (GR 349118) People did not remain in this high country without good reason. They used the passes to shorten their journeys but they got over them as quickly as possible. You have only to look at the landscape to the west of Patterdale village to understand how difficult the pack-horse trail over Grisedale Hause to Grasmere must have been. Only a few hardy farming families survived, until metal ores were Glenridding 🅿 ♿ ♨ found in the fells. Today, Glenridding looks like ∅ Mine [YHA >] any other small rural Lakeland village whose main concern is the holiday-maker. But, as you will find in other parts of the Lake District, many a settlement has quite a surprising past. Less than a mile up the steep-sided valley, whose straight alignment again tells of the scouring action of ice, lies the Greensides lead and silver mine. This is one of the easiest of all Lakeland's mines to visit. The path up slope through the village soon leads past former miners' cottages along the old miners' road towards the spoil heaps of the mine. These are a small

The northeastern fells 59

reminder of the smoke-blackened and noisy conditions from which this little valley suffered from the 18th century until just a few decades ago. Nevertheless, the old piece of wall, sluice or machine that you see cast carelessly over the fellside provides an evocative reminder of the past, when ore crushing, washing and smelting were carried out, first with water power and charcoal and later with coal.

Snow lies for an average of 120 days a year on Helvellyn's highest slopes and may still be seen in the shady north-east-facing hollows until July. As you look up into the dark and cavernous valleys that bite deep into Helvellyn's side, it is not too hard to imagine them filled with ice, the fellsides above bare and frost-riven, showering chips of rock on to the ice for transport to the lowlands.

At A5091 turn left for Keswick

Nothing that follows can match this grandeur, for you are now nearly back in slate country. One last area of tough volcanics remains, however, and forces the Aira beck to tumble and cascade down the valley side. Here, the famous Aira Falls point to yet another small valley left hanging above the main trough in which Ullswater now lies. There is a superb view back from the road as it climbs into this hanging valley, the whole of Helvellyn and the upper lakes encompassed in a single dramatic scene.

Walk 8

At the top of the climb lies Dockray, a small village that grew up around the power of water as it falls to the valley below. Here, woollen mills once flourished, their machines turned by the Aira beck, their raw material on the backs of sheep that walked the nearby fells. Today, the famous hardy Lakeland Herdwick sheep are the main visitors to the fells around the mine except in summer. Incidentally, they produce grey wool, so they are not as dirty as they may at first seem. By contrast, the village of Matterdale stands lonely in the wide, open centre of the fells. Here, there is not a fast-flowing stream in sight, and Matterdale relies entirely on agriculture for its survival.

[Keswick A66 >]

The road between Matterdale and Keswick provides broad, open vistas for the first time on this drive. Gone are the deep trenched valleys and the spectacular towering fells. Ahead and then on the right of the A66 lie the two largest of the broad hump-backed 'slate' fells – first Blencathra and then

(Opposite) **The broad back of Helvellyn rises dramatically from the road**

the mass of Skiddaw itself, standing guard over Keswick. Only above the village of Threkeld is there any sign of a craggy landscape – a sure sign that here the slates give way to a patch of tougher rocks.

At junction with B5322 turn left [St John in the Vale >] (🍴 etc. in Keswick 3 miles (4.8 km); town guide on Drive 3)

St John in the Vale brings you back into tough volcanic-rock country. As you travel south, this valley narrows like a funnel: the flat floor remains but the sides steepen and close until there is hardly room for the road alongside St John's Beck. Great Dodd soars high on the left and High Rigg to the right, but it is all too short and you suddenly come out into the wide expanse of Legburthwaitedale and the Thirlmere reservoir.

The whole of this unusual route through St John's Vale has been excavated along a belt of shattered rocks that marks the line where the Earth's crust once split and caused a tremendous earthquake. The long straight line of the rocks shows very clearly on a map and it controls the rest of your route back to Ambleside, for the shattered rocks have been eroded into low land.

At staggered junction cross A591 [Thirlmere >]

Legburthwaitedale is best seen from the west shore of Thirlmere. About a hundred years ago, people were still able to cross the natural lake by a short bridge to reach the little hamlet called Armboth by the side of this lake – that is, until Manchester started to run out of drinking water. In Legburthwaitedale there was a valley with steep sides and a narrow neck at one end: ideal for a reservoir. It seemed to the water engineers such a waste not to complete Nature's work by building a small dam at the northern end and flooding the valley. The first part of the lakeside drive goes over the dam and, by looking down to the right, you can see how small a structure was needed. Not that this comforted the people of Armboth, for their abandoned houses were rapidly covered by the rising reservoir level. At the northern end a sign still points to this long-forgotten village whose church bell is said still to toll beneath the waves.

Ice-scoured valleys are ideal for reservoirs because the dams needed to impound large amounts of water are so small. Fortunately, the reservoir treatment has not been applied to too many lakes, for you will notice that the penalties include prominent 'Keep out' signs and the extensive planting of whole hillsides of gloomy conifers. Originally, the conifers were established because people believed they would help shelter the soil in summer and reduce evaporation losses from the slopes that supply the reservoir with water. Sadly, scientists have recently discovered quite the reverse to be true; in fact the trees consume valuable water that would otherwise reach the lake.

Walk 7 Now, 100 years on, the reservoir has fitted fairly happily into the Lakeland scene and on still days its waters mirror the broad-backed ridge of Helvellyn to the east. This is not, however, Helvellyn's most attractive face: you see that on the road past Ullswater. In contrast to the deep shaded hollows Turn right [Ambleside A591 >] on the eastern flanks, here you see only a smooth, relatively unbroken, south-west facing slope. In the Ice Age this slope looked directly into the midday Sun, whose warming rays prevented snows from lingering long enough to form combs.

The main road continues its arrow-straight course southwards along the route etched out by ice in the zone of shattered rocks, rising to the head of Legburthwaitedale at the famous ice-breached pass of Dunmail Raise.

If ice had never been jammed into Legburthwaitedale, it would never have overspilled southwards to gouge out the breach in the fells that has proved so useful to generations of travellers. Perhaps, too, the fated day in AD 745, when Dunmail, King of Cumbria, went into battle against the King of Scotland, would not have occurred. Then, perhaps, he would never have been killed and his corpse buried under the cairn of stones (the raise) which lent its name to the pass.

Dunmail Raise is the last high spot on the route, deserving more time and attention than the fast-moving dual-carriageway traffic normally allows. As you drive past, however, do try to glance upwards to the frost-riven fells, their bare craggy slopes succumbing only slowly to the mellowing effects of grass and bracken.

When the ice moved southwards over Dunmail Raise, it again attacked the weakest rocks, eroding a sharply twisting valley that now contains the pretty lakes of Grasmere and Rydal Water. However, the lakes remain separated by a barrier of tough rock, a piece of which appears high on the left. This is Nab Scar, a cliff known as a truncated spur (*nab* = promontory), where glaciers sliced off the end of one of Fairfield's lengthy ridges. With this final reminder of the power of glacial action you return to the wooded confines of Ambleside.

3 The northwestern fells

Introduction

The northwestern fells are perhaps the most spectacular of Lakeland's fells to be viewed from the road. Seen from the Cumbrian coast they look especially grand, rising majestically from an area of much lower land made relatively featureless by a thick layer of material dumped by glaciers at the end of the Ice Age. In this drive you will see passes where ice has overriden mountains, cutting through whole fellsides like a knife through butter. In deep glaciated valleys you will find lakes of many forms, whose moods reflect the ever-changing weather: their surfaces sometimes ruffled and grey beneath a leaden sky; at other times crystal-clear and still, making perfect mirrors of the craggy fells towering above them. Here, too, are rapidly flowing streams and cascading waterfalls in profusion, some beside the road, others just pencil-thin streaks down a faraway fellside. Here traditional farming goes on hand in hand with tourism.

A figure-of-eight route: start at Keswick

The drive passes through much interesting landscape and you could use it as the start of a holiday to get your bearings. Keep an eye out, too, for the many character walks that begin along the route (Walks 1–6). Allow the best part of a day for this drive.

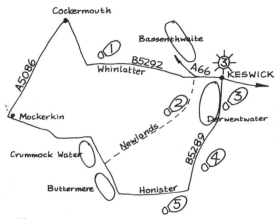

Drive 3: the northwestern fells

The route

Keswick 🅿 wc ♨ ♨ 🄿🄾 M ♨ 🄸 ∅ 🅼

Keswick, whose name means a place where cheese was made, is a natural focus of routes in the northern part of Lakeland. Now a town of some 6000, it lies in a wide pass dividing the broad, rounded back of Skiddaw from the main fells to the south. This easy, lowland route within the mountains has always encouraged movement inland from the coast. First the Romans (from their harbour of Maryport) and then the Vikings must have travelled this way, establishing settlements to take advantage of the fertile land that separates Derwentwater from Bassenthwaite lake. Later, the railway that was to bring tourists to Lakeland was built along the same route to connect Penrith (and thus the main line from London) to Workington and the coastal industrial towns. Today, the railway has gone, but the A66 trunk road that bypasses Keswick centre continues as the latest symbol of a long communications heritage.

Leave Keswick on A66 [Workington >]. In 3 miles (5 km), Braithwaite, turn left onto B5292 [Whinlatter Pass >]

Keswick is located on dry, sloping ground beside the River Greta, whose accumulating silt helped build the fertile land that now separates the two great lakes. Keswick is more than a place on a route: it is the place where roads from the fells in the south meet the roads of the lowland. Its easy access to markets beyond Lakeland made it the best place to manufacture cloth, using wool gathered from sheep grazing on the fellsides, or to make 'lead' pencils using graphite from the Borrowdale mines. Keswick has, consequently, always been the largest settlement of northern Lakeland.

Today, as you drive westwards out of Keswick, you can still see on your right the Cumberland Pencil Factory beside the River Greta. Once a roaring giant that drove the factory's machines, today the Greta is a relatively tame dwarf, carrying only such water as the North West Water Authority can spare from its Thirlmere reservoir.

The road to Braithwaite crosses the great fan of silt brought down from the fells by the rivers. Notice the dykes (walls) designed to protect the land from flooding, for this is land built by rivers.

From Braithwaite the road climbs steeply towards the fells, making for a deep pass once gouged out by a massive tongue of ice. However, you will not be aware of the pass until the final few yards before the summit, because the fellsides are thickly planted with conifers.

Along the way, numerous small quarries by the roadside show we are in 'slate' country. This type of 'slate' (made from old ocean muds) is not a tough rock, and although, in the past, glaciers have eroded steep slopes, already the work of frost has brought down a shower of rock chips to cover the bare rock and make a foundation for soil. At the

The northwestern fells 65

viewpoint there is a splendid outlook over the glacial trough in which Bassenthwaite now lies and beyond it the rounded fell of Skiddaw, its rocks the same as those by our roadside.

☆ (GR 224245) 🄿, picnic site on left in forest clearing

Beside the viewpoint and standing quite alone on the grass verge is an extraordinarily large boulder. Look at where someone in the past has thoughtlessly chipped and you will find it is a dark blotchy rock, an alien rock in a foreign land. In fact it is a piece of far-travelled volcanic rock left high on this hillside as a reminder of the tremendous carrying capacity of glaciers during the Ice Age. Along with many others still lying buried in the soil, this boulder was once used by the ice to erode the pass we are about to enter. Here, then, you get a glimpse of the hard rocks responsible for building the bold, craggy landscape to be seen ahead.

Forest visitor centre 🄿 M WC

The Whinlatter Pass is dark and forbidding for much of the year. Only in full sunlight does it brighten even a little. People have rarely dwelt long here and settlement is sparse. However, its vital role as a thoroughfare across the fells is plain enough, and soon the way opens out to Lorton Vale and lower land once more. Pack-horses used this pass for centuries, although their route followed the side of the valley opposite that taken by the 'new' motor road. The present road is therefore a sort of 'bypass', skirting the village of High Lorton.

Walk 1

At Lorton [Cockermouth >]

Cockermouth is a true lowland market town, trading goods from the plains with those from the fells. Today, this pleasant town is a good shopping and touring centre, but life for the townsfolk was not always so easy. Cockermouth was built in the easily defended tract of land between the rivers Cocker and Derwent. Market towns were rich, and first on the list for plundering! The town's defences were therefore completed by a castle, which is still well worth a visit, its limestone walls a reminder that here we are away from true Lakeland and on rocks that belong to the surrounding plain.

Cockermouth WC 🄿 ♥ 🛆 🏠 🄿🄾 M 🅸 ⊘ 🏛

Take A5086 [Egremont >]. In 5 miles (8 km) turn left [Mockerkin >] [Loweswater >] (3 ml; 5 km)

The road towards Egremont, Mockerin and Lowesdale runs over gently undulating land made from glacially dumped boulder clay, the solid rock largely buried. The mixture of arable and pasture fields also clearly belongs to a low land where the climate is drier than in the fells, and where the sunlight shines often enough for crops to ripen. This is a much richer land than the fells and it can support more people. Here, therefore, you will find many small hamlets and their network of narrow roads, so typical of good farmland and so alien to the fells.

Drives 66

As the road rises to give a view of Loweswater, you have nearly returned to the harsher world of the fells. These are not the rounded fells of slates that lay astride the Whinlatter Pass; they are bolder, craggy fells that owe their character to much tougher, volcanic rocks.

P 🥾 Hause Point

After a drive over country dominated by glacial deposition, Crummock Water is a reminder that, in the fells, glacial erosion is the dominant land-shaping process. Framing this beautiful lake are stark and deeply riven fells that culminate in High Stile (2644 ft; 806 m). Facing north-east, these fell-sides spend much of the day in shadow and they would have been one of the first places to nurture small glaciers in the Ice Age. Today, the result of glacial scouring has produced deep armchair-shaped hollows that now add diversity to this memorable scene.

Buttermere village 🛏
☕ **P** 🚻 **PO**

The village of Buttermere occupies the same type of position as Braithwaite. Here, too, streams have poured their debris into a lake, filling it up and making two lakes where once there was only one (p. 16).

Great scree slopes of frost-loosened rock mantle the fell below Mellbreak, Crummock Water

For the generations of farmers who succeeded the Vikings, these river-built lands have been a prize of incalculable value, allowing cattle to be grazed and grass to be cut for hay in an otherwise hostile environment. No wonder the Vikings called this 'the lake where butter could be made'.

The drive beside Buttermere becomes somewhat claustrophobic as the valley head is approached. On the left is the broad swell of Robinson (2417 ft; 737 m); on the right, across the lake, High Stile and the ridge called Haystacks. Ahead the prow-shaped mass of Fleetwith Pike (2126 ft; 648 m) rears ever larger. Finally, when it seems that the way ahead is completely blocked by towering, frost-riven crags, the road sweeps left and the awesome valley of the Honister Pass lies before you.

🅿 at Pass 1176 ft (358 m), Walk 5

Honister Pass is one of the most impressive sights in Lakeland. You should certainly take time to stop at its foot and admire the gracefully sweeping lines of the valley and the fells, which, on both sides, seem to climb straight up into the sky. Here, too, a little stone bridge reminds you that this pass has an ancient history and that you are following in the footsteps of many generations of pack-horse teams.

Ahead on both left and right, the fellsides are cloaked in a chain-mail of rock chips that once tumbled down from the frosted slopes above. This is only a superficial cover that tells of a late stage in the history of this valley, for like all other Lakeland passes, this is the work of a tongue of ice that once probed between valleys.

The summit car park lies beside the Honister quarries whose spoil is strewn haphazardly over the landscape. Here, the volcanic rocks have been exploited because they readily split into sheets and make good roofing slates. Although it is the quarry that first attracts the eye, together with the panorama back to Buttermere, it is also worth wandering from the car park northwards into the Pass head, for here we enter a world like that of the great Alpine passes. Barren of all but a smattering of glacial debris, this ice-smoothed scene exhibits vegetation rarely seen in Lakeland. With the cold wind frequently whistling over the pass, and boggy conditions prevailing, only tiny herbs grow here, their delicate flowers scattered among what at first appears as a uniform grey–green grass mat.

(Opposite) **Honister Pass, its U shape highlighted by a band of sunlight: Fleetwith Pike on the left, Dale Head on the right (view looking south)**

Almost as soon as you crest the pass, the road twists and bends down to Borrowdale. Down this slope (which today requires a low gear and a foot constantly on the brake) quarrymen once hauled slates on rough wooden sledges to the valley below. It is said that one man once made 17 journeys in a day – uphill as well as down!

The road reaches Borrowdale at only 340 ft (104 m) above sea level, a descent from the pass of some 800 ft (244 m) in about 1 mile (1.6 km). When you reach the bottom, the contrast could not be greater, for the road runs over flat land that was once the bed of a lake. Nevertheless, the whole valley and the lake basin of Derwentwater are almost entirely the work of erosion. Here you do not find the wild and hostile landscape of Honister because the shelter provided by the valley has allowed trees to grow and has helped to soften the harsh rock outlines. Johnny's Wood, one of the natural oak woods that escaped the woodman's axe, and now in the safe keeping of the National Trust, has remained sufficiently large to show what the whole valley must once have looked like.

Johnny's Wood on valley side opposite Seatoller

Flood-level posts beside the road tell you that the former lake area between Rosthwaite and Seatoller sometimes reverts to a lake even today. Only once or twice does the road rise and fall over ridges of glacial debris, although the nearby Bowder Stone – a huge boulder left high on the fellside by a glacier – reminds us how large the glaciers must have been. To the north the valley narrows into the 'Jaws of Borrowdale', a gap so narrow that no debris has survived the winnowing powers of water and where all the rocks are clean and bare. The gap is due to an extremely tough rock band that has resisted the erosive power of ice, keeping the valley narrow and its sides almost sheer. Yet the restriction is only temporary for, beyond the Jaws, the valley widens once again as you at last turn towards the bright waters of Derwentwater.

Bowder Stone 🅿

It is worth stopping at Grange, just beyond the Jaws. Here, a little stone bridge has been built where the Derwent is contained between a rock knoll and the fellside. The knoll is an upstanding piece of the valley floor that has resisted bulldozing by the ice, although its surface remains covered with deep, ice-scoured grooves. This knoll probably determined the position of Grange because the village grew up where crossing the river was easiest.

Grange ⊟ 🅿 wc 🅿

Grange also marks the start of the famous

Grange in Borrowdale: the fell of High Spy is the backdrop

Derwentwater lake, although you may not think so if you stand on the bridge looking down stream. But, in fact, the land before you is simply the silted-up lake end. Here, the river once entered the lake, although today open water is more than a mile away, opposite the Lodore Hotel, a clear example of the way all the region's lakes are slowly being filled in. The village bridge is a good place for looking up at the fells, because there is a clear contrast between the rounded forms to the west and the stark, craggy slopes to the east. As you follow the road on towards Keswick, this contrast continues; across the lake are the weak 'slates' that you saw at the start of the drive, and beside you are the tough volcanics that have provided the most dramatic fells along your route. In fact the junction between these two rock types lies beneath the road.

Route variations
The route described here is worth more than one visit. However, to vary the scene, an alternative is to drive from Braithwaite along Newlands valley (signposted to Buttermere).

The northwestern fells 71

Walks of fell, dale and coast

1 A jewel in the forest: Spout Force, Whinlatter Pass

Introduction

Not all the valleys in the Lake District are rugged clefts between craggy mountains. The northern fells in particular are made of slates that are easily eroded into rounded summits, such as Skiddaw and Blencathra. However, for the very reason that the Whinlatter Pass area is carved from these relatively soft rocks, it is all the more surprising to find one of the symbols of tough rock – a spectacular waterfall – set deep amid evenly rounded fells.

At first sight, the route to Spout Force is not at all promising. There is simply a large signpost inviting you to follow the old quarry track beside a stream. The route itself is shrouded in a gloomy mantle of tall spruce and larch trees. However, do not be put off by this forbidding vista, for the valley has much of interest to offer.

The walks

🚗 from Keswick, A66 west, then B5292 [Whinlatter >]. Spout Force is 1 mile (1.6 km) after summit

(a) Short and easy. Follow **1,2,3** and return by the same route (45 minutes).

(b) Slightly more energetic and longer. Follow **1,2, 3,4** and complete the circular trip (1½ hours).

The route

1 There is something unusual about the little valley of Aiken Beck. Notice how the quarrymen have scarred the left side of the valley but have completely ignored the right. See also how the left valley side is so much steeper than the right. Furthermore, landslides in the right bank expose a tenacious mixture of boulders, pebbles and clay – the tell-tale signs of glacial deposits – whereas on the left side there is strikingly little material.

If you pick up a piece of the quarry spoil, you will see that it splits into reasonably thin sheets that make good roofing slates. Such material is rare in the Lakes and its occurrence in this exposed position is the reason for all the quarrying.

In this lower section of the valley there is very little solid rock to be seen in the stream bed, and the stream tends to meander over a pebbly floor. This is because, as the stream twists and turns, undercutting its banks, the soft boulder clay collapses and there is a continuous supply of pebbles and boulders to the stream bed. Above the steepened

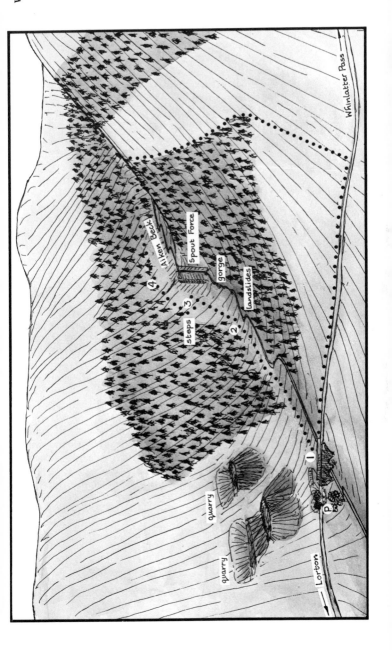

Whinlatter Pass

Aiken Beck

Spout Force

gorge

landslides

steps

3

2

4

1

quarry

quarry

P

Lorton

banks, landslides are common, especially where the foresters have left gaps (rides) in the conifer plantation, depriving the soil of its stabilising root 'anchors'.

Although there are many signs of glacial erosion in the form of boulder clay in the river bed and plastered over the valley sides, these are not matched by a wide-bottomed glacially eroded valley because this little side valley could not push its ice stream out into the main glacier that flowed over Whinlatter. Ice from the main valley may instead have forced its way up the tributary from time to time. The result has been widespread deposition but relatively little apparent erosion.

2 ✳ Waterfall

The most striking feature of the walk is the sudden appearance of Spout Force through an opening in the trees where the Forestry Commission have thoughtfully provided a splendid viewpoint. Above the waterfall the river meanders as though completely unaware of the fate in store, then suddenly plunges over a lip and down a vertical face to dash itself against the rocks in the gorge below.

3 Steps lead up slope

A close (but *not recommended*) inspection of the lip of the waterfall would show that the rock forming the upper ledge is a sill. This formerly molten material was injected between layers of shale during the time when the volcanic rocks of central Lakeland were in the making. To either side of the waterfall the valley is also much narrower than stretches above or below, another reflection of the toughness of the band of lava.

4

The wide, gentle valley up stream from the waterfall is best seen by catching brief glimpses through the mass of conifers. A helpfully placed stone seat provides a resting- and viewing-point in this steep section. From here you can see how the chance location of a thin band of tough rock can be so important in forming a landscape, providing interest and variety in this short walk.

Return by same route or follow circular footpath that gives views over Swinside

(Opposite) **Spout Force cascades over a band of tough rock into a gorge as high as the spruce trees**

2 The miners' road: Stonycroft Gill, near Braithwaite

Introduction

The spacious valley that contains Derwentwater was produced not by a single stream but by the combined power of many rivers of ice, each flowing from its own small valley but gathering in the Derwent to surge onwards to the north-west. Several tributary valleys still descend quite steeply to the Derwent. They contain much of interest and offer some of the best views in Lakeland. This route follows an old miners' trail up the valley of Stonycroft Gill, rising to reach the fells at a saddle and giving the walker a striking panorama of Lakeland scenery for the minimum of effort.

The walks

➔ from Keswick, A66 west to Braithwaite [Buttermere and Newlands valley >] 🅿 1 mile (1.6 km) on right beyond quarry

(a) Short and easy. Follow **1,2,3** and return (1 hour).

(b) Longer but has a good view over the mine. Follow **1,2,3,4** and return (2–3 hours).

(c) A fell-top walk for those with a fair head for heights, who seek an even finer view. Follow **1,2,3,4,5** (half a day).

The route

1 The lower valley of Stonycroft Gill has been eroded in the relatively soft shaly rock that characterises most of the northern fells. It is easily shattered when exposed to frost and is readily rotted by rain water to make soils. As a result, the solid rock is rarely seen on the surface at all. The large scree slopes beside the road were produced quickly by frost action in the brief cold period while glaciers were finally melting away. Since that time the screes have become stabilised and buried beneath a protective cover of soil, grass and bracken. However, the skin of the soil and vegetation is very fragile and its hold on the fellside easily broken.

As man came to this area to tend his animals and later to mine ores, he was, at first, resigned to the need to travel mainly along spongy valley bottoms. However, tracks must have become sodden and virtually impassable in winter. Eventually, all-weather routes were needed, and this meant digging deep into the fellsides and, especially, cutting into the easily excavated screes. The rocks that once bounced down from the frost-riven upper slope to make the screes are almost ideal for road metal: they are easy to quarry, need no blasting and, most important of all, they are on the spot. Today, quarrying has ceased but above the quarry a 'knock-on' effect has developed as material slithers

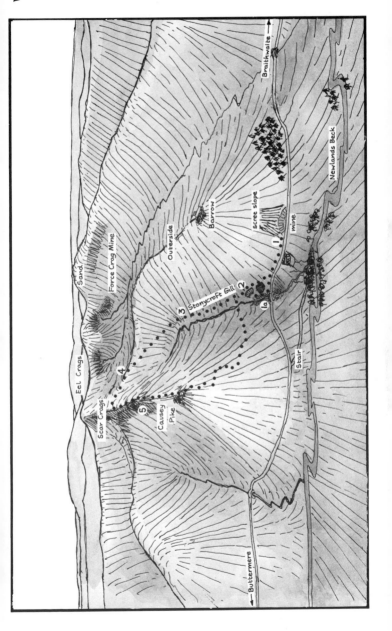

Buttermere

Eel Crags

Sand.

Force Crag Mine

Stonycroft Gill

Outerside

Barrow

scree slope

mine

Scar Crags

Causey Pike

Stair

Newlands Beck

Braithwaite

sporadically down hill, falling on to the quarry floor. In time the quarry will be filled and the slope will be covered with soil and vegetation once again. At present, however, scars show where large areas of soil have been stripped away and with it the grass on which grazing depends.

1a Follow farm track rising from road right (easy ascent) or go to bridge and walk up stream on right bank

The small stone bridge carrying the road across the beck is little more than a strengthened pack-horse bridge. As so often in Lakeland, this has been built strategically across a small rocky gorge where a firm footing is provided on both banks. It is a good place for a picnic, and nearby you can look out on a scene of classic rural tranquillity, of lowland pasture and upland fell.

The hamlet and fields would not have looked at all like this in earlier centuries. For instance, just below the road, the tiny hamlet of Stair was dominated by the sounds from its woollen mill until less than a hundred years ago; for centuries before that, even the splash of water tumbling under the bridge would have been drowned by the crash of water-driven hammers, and the view would have been marred by smoke belching from furnaces on its banks. It takes a keen eye to find any trace of these industries now. The easiest to see are the grey spoil heaps of the now abandoned Uzicca mine next to the roadside quarry. However, by following the Gill up stream, further tantalising glimpses of the past are revealed. The rough and partly overgrown channel cut in the rock just a few steps above the bridge is an artificial watercourse leading from the Gill to the mine. If you follow it to the stream bank, there are the post-holes and iron bolts that are sure signs of a diversion dam.

This was a good place to choose to divert water for power, for here the Stonycroft Gill flows swiftly down into the much larger Newlands valley. But what did the miners or the bridge-builders make of the little gorge they found so useful? They would certainly not have known that it marks the site of a bar of hard rock cut by a stream carrying waters away from a melting glacier higher up the valley. As you walk up slope there is further evidence of this former glacier.

2 The 'farm' track running parallel to the right bank was made and used by miners several centuries ago, and the spoil beside the track shows where

(Opposite) **View from 2 over Derwentwater: Bleaberry Fell behind the lake and Great Dodd (Ullswater) in the distance; the near fell on the right is Cat Bells**

they once stocked huge piles of rock containing metal ores from the fellside above, and then roasted them in a jacket of charcoal to separate metal from rock. If you look among the spoil, you will find the black glassy rock that was part of the slag formed by the roasting. A little further up stream there are even the remains of an old dam used to divert water from the stream bed, and of a mineral vein that followed the course of the stream. Today, it is difficult to imagine what the ugly scene must have looked like.

3   The valley takes a straight – and therefore glacially cut – route down from the fells, and you can see the miners' track sweep along, following the Gill with only a single curve to the left. Beneath your feet are the flaky blue shales of the quarry. However, when you draw level with the knob of bare rock that caps the fell to the left (Causey Pike), the colour changes to the grey–green volcanic rocks typical of the central fells.

Causey Pike marks the junction between the weak and the tough rocks. Indeed, with its craggy profile set against the sky, the Pike is the most northerly outpost of the central fells. Ahead, the view is changing fast as you leave behind the smooth fellsides and get a first glimpse of the high fell country.

4   As you walk further along the track, it gradually becomes obvious that Stonycroft Gill occupies a valley that has no proper 'head', for the track has been splendidly engineered to reach a saddle-shaped gap (or col) in the ridge ahead. From this gap you can now see the majestic central fells them-selves, their craggy, rough outlines rising sharply up from the valley below. You now stand at the lowest point of a 'bite' taken out of the ridge by ice spilling over from one valley into another. In fact you are in a smaller and higher version of Dunmail Raise or Kirkstone Pass.

Take time to look around the fells, but then glance down into the valley ahead, for there, like a speck of dust on a painting, is Force Crag Mine. At present, the miners excavate barytes, but in earlier years mining was concerned strictly with metal ores. Above the modern mine lie the ruins of the old workings, now only derelict brick buildings and spoil heaps. All mining here, deep into the rock following ore veins, was by horizontal tunnels (adits) whose entrances can still be seen from your vantage point if you use binoculars.

Above the old mine stands another saddle-shaped col where ice poured across a formerly high divide. The miners' road, however, heads off left towards a mine even more remote than that of Force Crag. Today, there is little sign of the mine at Scar Crags, but the track continues upwards towards it across a scree slope, making for a low point in the ridge ahead. (*Note:* the scree can be avoided by walking directly up the fell side from the saddle.) At the ridge top the miners' road is lost, but now you get your reward for the exertion of the last few hundred yards. Away to the south-east is the broad back of Helvellyn, to the north the rounded hump of Skiddaw, and to the south-west the central fells, culminating in Scafell and the Gables. From here, too, there is a bird's-eye view of the deep, straight, glaciated valleys. You can also see how close these glaciers came to destroying the ridge on which you stand. The ridge may not be as sharp as the famous Striding Edge on Helvellyn but its steep sides are a dramatic testimony to the erosive powers of ice. This ridge is also a place from which to survey the miners' route. As you walk along, encumbered with perhaps nothing heavier than a light waterproof, consider the plight of the miners as they pulled the ore on sledges from the mountain-tops down to the smelter below, with little time to look at the landscape around them.

Return to 1 by following the ridge crest using the well worn track.

3 The hanging valley: Lodore Falls and the Watendlath valley

Introduction

The Lodore Falls can be placed among the half dozen most renowned places in the Lake District. Along with the nearby Bowder Stone, the Falls (or, more accurately, the Cascades) are an essential halt for coach parties. Another classic tourist halt is Surprise View near the pack-horse bridge at Ashness. These three tourist attractions have one thing in common: all were formed by glaciers. Surprise View looks out from the lip of a hanging valley into the deep trench of Borrowdale and Derwentwater; the Lodore Cascades complete the precipitous journey of water between hanging valley and lake; and the Bowder Stone rests precariously on the valley side where it was left as glaciers melted away. It is possible to visit both Surprise View and the Lodore Cascades, together with the more imposing Lodore Falls, by an easy walk toward Watendlath that also takes you away from the lakeside crowds and into pleasant woods. An attractive walk reaches the Bowder Stone.

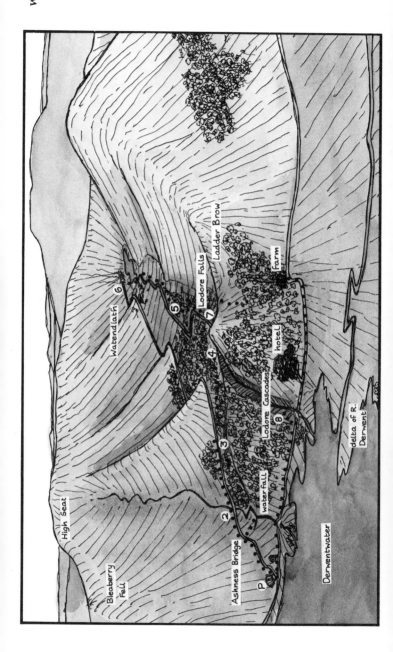

High Seat

Bleaberry Fell

Watendlath

Ladder Brow

Lodore Falls

6

5

7

4

3

2

waterfall

Lodore Cascades

8

Askness Bridge

P

hotel

farm

delta of R. Derwent

Derwentwater

The walks

🚶 from Keswick,
B5289 [Borrowdale
>]. In 2 miles
(3.1 km) turn left
[Ashness >]
🅿 on left

(a) Short and easy, to see Ashness Bridge, Lodore Cascades and Surprise View. Follow **2,3,1,8** (parking beyond **2** to save the uphill walk) (1½ hours).

(b) To include Lodore Falls and part of the Watendlath valley, no steep tracks and mainly on well made paths. Follow **1,2,3,4,7,8** (half a day).

(c) Longer, to include a visit to remote Watendlath. Follow **1** through to **8**. No more than a moderately steep descent on a good track and mostly flat. Most of a day; take your sandwiches.

The route

Ashness and Watendlath are two hamlets tucked away high above Borrowdale in a valley left hanging after the recent Ice Age. While a powerful glacier surged down from the fells near Great Gable at the head of Borrowdale, cutting the deep trench in which Derwentwater now lies, a small tongue of ice in the Watendlath valley was shut in, a virtual prisoner, unable to escape into Borrowdale because of the mass of ice already there. As a result there was far less scouring and the valley floor was left hanging higher and higher as Borrowdale was constantly deepened. With the ice gone, the Watendlath Gill can now only reach Borrowdale by means of falls and cascades, which come tumbling down the steep, craggy side.

1 Quarry 🅿 walk up
hill, then cross to
stream right. Follow
footpath beside
stream down hill to
waterfall

When the Victorians discovered Lakeland as a pleasant retreat, they had a keen eye for finding the best sites for their houses. Barrow House, now a youth hostel, can just be seen from the road, half hidden among the trees on the right. Placed on the highest point of the delta built out into Derwentwater by the Barrow beck, its gardens had the delight of a waterfall (which has been subsequently modified to make it more spectacular) and a supply of fresh water. Water is still taken from this stream through a gravel sink behind the small dam overlooking the waterfall.

The road to Ashness takes a diagonal route to reach the Watendlath valley some 500 ft (152 m) above Derwentwater while keeping as even a gradient as possible. Ahead and to the left, Bleaberry Fell (1932 ft; 589 m) dominates the skyline, its rough profile telling of the tough volcanic rocks that underlie the area. More directly ahead lies neighbouring High Seat (1996 ft; 608 m).

Lodore Falls and the Watendlath valley 85

2 Ashness Bridge   Ashness once lay on the lonely fell 'road' from
Keswick to Ambleside that climbed into the
Watendlath valley, then over Armboth Fell before
descending, via Dunmail Raise, a track followed by
drovers with trains of mules carrying packs. To
cross the Barrow beck a sturdy stone bridge was
built, today visited by thousands of holiday-
makers, since it is from here that you get your first
view back over Derwentwater.

3 Surprise View   A panorama somewhat less restricted by trees is
that from Surprise View, where the road returns to
the lip of Borrowdale, here made completely sheer
by the scouring of the ancient glaciers.

From these vantage points above the lake, a
superb panorama opens up, revealing Derwentwater framed by the distant summits of Skiddaw
and neighbouring fells. Look below this apparently
timeless scene where the River Derwent pours into
the lake. You will clearly see that subtle changes are
at work even as you watch, for Derwentwater is
gradually silting up with material brought by the
swift river. The long fingers of sediment that have
pushed out into the lake are clearly revealed
through shallow waters (something impossible to
see from the shore itself). The wide expanse of flat
marshy land indicates just how much progress has
already been made.

[Watendlath >]   By the time the viewpoint is reached, the road
footpath to   has lost its steep gradient and now dodges between
footbridge   large, glacially smoothed outcrops of rock. Each
groove on these rocks bears witness to a boulder
once embedded in the underside of a glacier that
gouged a path across the floor of the Watendlath
valley. Here you are in the hanging valley itself, a
wooded wilderness of green, lichen-hung trees and
spongy moss-covered ground that casts an all-
pervading eerie atmosphere. Finally, the trees part
and the Watendlath dale comes into view, its
grassy floor wide and open like· some long-
forgotten Alpine valley.

4 Route choice: At the bridge over the Watendlath beck you can
longer (5,6,7)   wander up stream along the floor of the valley to
Watendlath hamlet. If you do, you will be beside a
5 stream that seems to be in lowland, as it meanders
across the flat floor of this glaciated valley, which
rises by no more than 25 ft (7.6 m) in nearly a mile.
Nevertheless, with steep fells on either side, the
origin of this splendid and quiet valley is clear.

6   Beyond the tiny, rugged stone-built hamlet of

(Opposite) **Watendlathdale with Armboth Fell in the distance**

Lodore Falls and the Watendlath valley   87

Watendlath, you may care to pause beside the tarn – a tiny patch of water held up behind a bar of particularly tough rock – and look up to Armboth Fell on the left and to the broad mass of Ullscarf at the valley head. Slightly to the left of Ullscarf lies Blea Tarn and the vantage point of Walk 6. (*Note:* a footpath from the far side of the tarn leads to the Bowder Stone, although this is more conveniently reached from the main Borrowdale road.)

Shorter (7)

Within a few yards of the edge of the woods, the stream tumbles out of sight leaving the footpath to follow some long-abandoned channel between high walls of rock.

7 [Lodore Falls >]

The Lodore Falls comprise several stages, with water alternately falling and cascading over a collection of rocks of varied hardness, which make up the lip of the hanging valley. For the most part, the beck follows a deep and narrow gorge that was probably cut when melting waters were still confined to narrow tunnels beneath the wasting sheets of ice.

Path beside stream on right bank very steep; path on left even worse. Follow easy track down over Ladder Brow to main road, then turn tight

It seems likely that the present course of the Watendlath beck, as it leaves the upper falls and turns sharply right towards the Lodore Cascades, is a relatively recent one, because an alternative exit of the Watendlath valley into Borrowdale is over the broad saddle of Ladder Brow. However, although a glacier may have been able to force its way over Ladder Brow to join the trunk glacier of the main valley, stream water cannot flow up hill, and the Watendlath beck has subsequently had to circumvent Ladder Brow by cutting a defile along a narrow line of weakness.

8 Lodore Cascades turn right *after* Lodore Hotel through woods **WC**

The Lodore Cascades are quite different from the high-level Lodore Falls, even though the two are frequently assumed to be the same. Behind the Lodore Hotel, the Watendlath beck finally tumbles over and between huge boulders that choke the river gorge. This is not a true waterfall, but an especially steep section of the river, whose boulder-choked path forces the water to perform a series of short acrobatics. Most of these boulders are now incapable of being moved by even the greatest of storms. Thus, they must be a heritage of the closing stages of the Ice Age, probably brought hurtling down by some ferocious torrent beneath a melting glacier as it plunged into Borrowdale.

(Opposite) **Derwentwater from the lakeside near the Lodore Hotel**

From Cascades keep
to footpath in woods
parallel to road and
return to **1**

The final walk back from the Cascades is through coppiced woodland, once used for charcoal. There are also some recent plantings and the small girth of the tree trunks shows that few have been growing for more than 30 or 40 years. Beneath them grows a thicket of ivy, blackberry and other undergrowth, the first colonisers of new ground. Even this thick growth cannot totally conceal the extensive screes of huge angular boulders that create a steep ramp up from the roadside to the vertical wall of the main valley side. Formed just after the end of the Ice Age, but while conditions were still cold enough to cause enormous quantities of rock to be prised from the valley walls by frost, today the screes are slowly being covered with vegetation and are weathering into soil. Eventually they will disappear from view completely – unless, of course, we enter another Ice Age.

4   Where all roads cross: Seathwaite and Sty Head

Introduction
This walk takes us to the central fells, a distinctive area with its high and rugged crags, a harsh and uncompromising landscape where even the hardy Lakeland sheep keep to the low ground. Yet to appreciate the character of these fells does not require great walking experience. The loftiness of the peaks can be seen from the shelter of the valleys, as the route from Seathwaite shows. For more energetic readers we also include a venture to the 'Crossroads of the Lakes' at Sty Head.

The walks

🚗 from Keswick,
B5289 [Borrowdale
>]. In 5 miles (8 km)
[Seathwaite >] on
left. 🅿 at end

(a) Short and easy along flat ground. Follow **1,2, 3,4** to Stockley Bridge and return (1½ hours).
(b) For those tempted further along a moderately easy path. Follow **1,2,3,4,10,9,8** and return (the best part of a morning).
(c) For those who do not mind a stiff uphill walk. Follow **1,2,3,4,5,6,7** and return (also the best part of a morning).
(d) For the energetic. Follow **1** through to **10** but give yourself all day, take a packed lunch and take heed of any local weather warnings.

The route
Seathwaite is built at the upper limit of cultivable land. It is a true fell-land site, with small pastures below and rough grazing above. It could never have provided more than a harsh existence for the generations of farmers who have survived here. Remember that you are probably seeing it in summer: come back and take another look in

Walks 90

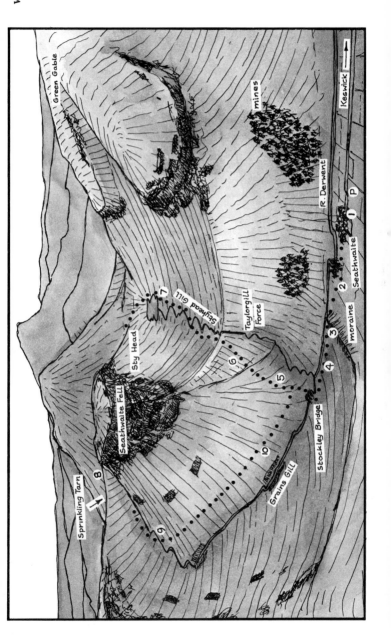

Green Gable

mines

Keswick →

R. Derwent

P

Seathwaite

1

2

moraine

3

Taylorgill Force

Styhead Gill

7

Sty Head

Seathwaite Fell

6

4

5

Stockley Bridge

10

Grains Gill

9

Sprinkling Tarn

8

January, if you can get there! Seathwaite is also notorious for having the highest annual rainfall in England, so do not be too disappointed if some of the 120 in (3050 mm) is falling when you pay it a visit.

As soon as you leave your car, look back along the road over which you have come and see how flat the ground is – quite a surprise for such an otherwise mountainous environment. Notice, too, how the dry-stone walls are made from the partly rounded boulders so characteristic of glacial debris.

1 Follow broad track through farmyard

For a change, most of the boulders for these walls were picked not from the fields but from the nearby river, for here the fields are naturally boulder-free because they are on the bed of an old lake, long since disappeared with the glacial debris that impounded it. Such fine silty soil is rare in the Lakes and it is a particularly treasured possession here.

As soon as you go through the farmyard you are faced with a totally different landscape. Gone are the fields and flat land; in their place, within a few yards at least, is a valley floor strewn with boulders and a tumbling river that continually searches its rocky bed for any small particle to wash away. The valley slope is noticeably steeper too, although it hardly makes for difficult walking.

2 Just beyond the small conifer plantation you may care to leave the track and venture a few feet to the left, up on to the grassy slopes where you get a clear view back over the valley. From here, the farm and cottages appear to hide on one side of the valley floor as far from the turbulent stream as possible. Above the farm and to the left is a waterfall dashing the waters of Sour Milk Gill against the rocks of the valley floor. Half-way up the opposite slope are the graphite mines that once put the 'lead' in Keswick's 'Cumberland pencils'.

Closer at hand, the bank of boulders in their steel cages is a reminder that winter storms and melting snows can turn an erstwhile pretty stream into a raging torrent. Without this protection the conifers would not survive for long.

3 A little further up stream the path picks its way through a strange, hummocky landscape. Seen from the stream bank, the tell-tale chaos of boulders and clays shows this to be the last vestige of material left by a glacier. At the moment it covers only half the valley, but did the debris once block

(Opposite) **View from 2: here, ice-eroded boulders remain to dominate the valley floor, while the fine materials have been washed away, and piles of boulder clay, as yet unworked by the stream, mantle the fellside just ahead of the walkers**

the valley completely, damming up a small lake that finally overtopped this embankment, washing half of it away? If this was the case, then some of the boulders in the stream may bear silent witness to this ancient event.

4   The valley ahead is a wide open U shape, showing all the signs of glacial erosion. Off to the right, the waterfall of Taylorgill Force provides a pencil-thin cascade of foam to show where the small valley beyond hangs high above its master valley.

Choice of routes at Stockley Bridge

The builders of Stockley Bridge have also highlighted the effects of glacial erosion because they have built their little stone structure over a gorge
5   cut through solid rock. This bridge also leads you straight towards an exposed part of the valley side that illustrates both the typical scratch marks of glacial scouring and the sharp angular faces where lumps of rock have been torn right off the floor by the passing ice.

The best view of the lower valley is from the
6   gaping jaws of the hanging valley above. It is easier from this vantage point to imagine the lake beyond the farm, the ice sheet that pushed debris up into the hummocks by the river, the glacier that carved the valley, and the intense frost that shattered the fellside rocks, sending them cascading as screes on to the valley side.

You can also look down on to the tumbling waters of Taylorgill Force, but its apparent erosive strength is misleading, for it has made little impression on the hanging valley side created by ice 10000 or more years ago. Like all the streams today, it is but a shadow of its predecessors.

Beyond this point make sure you have a good local map and adequate clothing

The land above the waterfall is a different world from the valley below. You will most probably be greeted by a wind, welcoming at first, after the stiff walk, but chilling if you sit for any length of time.
7   Around you the vegetation is almost Alpine in character, which is perhaps not surprising in a valley overlooked by some of Lakeland's highest summits. Straight ahead is the highest point in England, Scafell Pike (3206 ft; 977 m) surrounded by other craggy giants. Off to the right is the lonely, broad back of Great Gable (2949 ft; 899 m) and, separated from it by a dip aptly named Windy Gap, is its smaller neighbour, Green Gable (2527 ft; 770 m). To the left the bulk of Great End (2984 ft; 910 m) dominates the skyline. Cradled within these majestic fells is Sty Head Tarn in its glacially

(Opposite) **The old flat lake bed beyond Seathwaite from near Taylorgill Force (6)**

scooped hollow. Behind lies the saddle called Sty Head, the broken remnant of a rocky ridge that once connected Great Gable to Great End. This ridge has long since been eroded into its present subdued form when ice pushed northwards from Scafell.

The route runs round the back of the tarn and then via Sty Head through yet another saddle towards Sprinkling Tarn, a higher-level twin of Sty Head Tarn. From above Sprinkling Tarn you can see that you are standing in a line of saddles making a relatively low-level 'trench' set among the mountains that make the roof of England. This 'corridor' is eroded in a belt of rocks once shattered by an ancient earthquake and therefore an easy prey to the scouring action of moving ice.

8 ☆ The upper part of Grains Gill valley contains hummocky land of boulder clay pushed into shape by the last fitful advance of a retreating glacier some 8000 years ago. Ahead the valley opens out quickly to give the magnificent view that leads through the valley of Grains Gill over Seathwaite towards Borrowdale in the distance. This remarkably straight route could only be the work of a glacial bulldozer, a vast mass of ice that tore and scraped at the old river valley until spurs of land had been sliced off and a wide course opened out.

9 Beyond the little bridge lie more piles of boulder clay. Unfortunately, the material has not withstood the tread of many feet and it is eroding badly along the line of the track. Looking like grey spoil heaps from ancient mines, mounds of boulder clay running along the valley side provide a measure of the height of the ice the last time it occupied the valley. If you draw an imaginary line across the valley to join up these deposits, you will see that the valley was filled to a depth of several hundred feet.

When the ice melted some 12 000 years ago, the
10 power of meltwater laden with newly eroded debris would have been considerably greater than that of an ordinary stream. The contrast shows particularly clearly if you venture carefully towards the stream (which is out of sight of the track at this point). The gorge in which the present river flows was cut almost entirely by water from a melting glacier.

5 Stockley Bridge is a fine place to pause after a stint of hard walking on the fells. At the junction of the two tributary valleys, it is also a good point from which to gain a perspective of all the landscape features before strolling back to the car.

5 The roof of England: Fleetwith Pike and Green Gable

Introduction

Drives through central Lakeland valleys give tantalising glimpses of fells towering out of sight. The panoramic views from the fell-tops can be breathtaking, yet they seem inaccessible to all but the most ardent of hill walkers. However, just occasionally, the Lakeland roads rise high enough to make access to the fell-tops fairly easy. One of the most popular walks from a high-level pass begins at Honister Pass, from whence you can quickly reach the roof of England.

from Keswick, B5289 [Borrowdale >]. Ascend pass, ⓟ at summit

The walks

(a) Moderately easy, first following a quarry road, then a well trodden path across the fell summit. Follow **1,2,3,4** and return (2 hours).

(b) Longer, to look down from Green Gable to the head of Borrowdale. Follow **1,2,3,4,5** (half a day).

(c) For the more energetic the scramble up to Great Gable, probably the most popular high summit in Lakeland. Follow **1** through to **6**. This takes most of a day: take your sandwiches. Always take heed of the local weather forecast.

The route

Fleetwith Pike is a steep-sided westward projection from the mass of tough volcanic rocks that culminate in Great Gable. Originally formed as layers of volcanic ash and lava beneath an ancient sea, these rocks were heaved up and stood on their sides as part of the great earth movements that formed the central Lake District. Slowly the elements of the weather combined forces to etch out lines of weaker rock and turn them into broad, open valleys. Throughout this time, Honister Pass did not exist because the solid rock ridge connecting Fleetwith Pike with Dale Head (on the western side of Honister Pass) was still unbroken. There were probably two small valleys leading from Honister, one to the south and the other to the north, but they had hardly succeeded in producing a pass. Only when the Ice Age came to Lakeland did Honister begin to form. At a point now high above the road there must have been a low-lying saddle in the fells. Across this, ice spilled, grinding and tearing at the rock and producing in a few tens of thousands of years what rivers had failed to achieve in tens of millions.

1 Walk through quarry yard and up quarry track

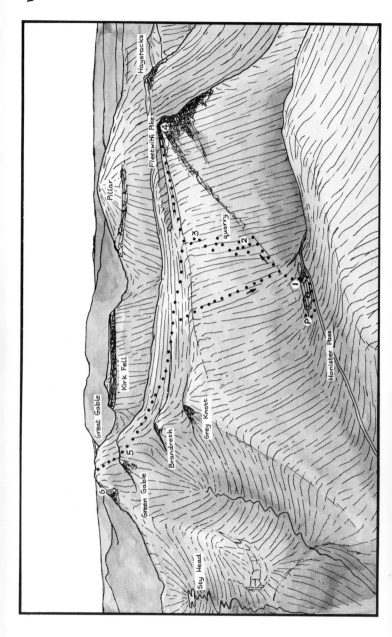

As you walk up the quarry road, the spectacular evidence of glaciation is all around: in the sweeping U shape of the Pass; in the humps of glacial debris now left littering the floor of Honister north of the summit; in the chaos of bouldery debris that has been uncovered by countless feet as they make their way towards Great Gable; and in the ice-smoothed rocks that project through the soil along the way.

It may seem incredible that the whole of this dramatic pass is such a recent arrival in the landscape, but there is much that is even younger. The departure of ice from the valleys a mere 12 000 years ago did not herald a return to the present relatively mild climate, because the weather remained bitterly cold. Frost continued to bite deeply into the bare rock, causing it to shatter into flakes, which fell towards the valley floor. Over hundreds of years these splinters slid and bounced, each one coming to rest in such a way as to form the vast screes now littering the lower slopes. Although most of these rocks are a result of Nature's own quarrying, some of the freshest, green-coloured screes are the result of the work of man, for here, in one relatively thin bed, is a rock made from volcanic ash that will split easily into fine roofing slates.

In some ways, Nature has not been kind to the quarryman, for the rock they seek lies high up on the precipitous sides of the Pass; yet, but for the work of ice, it might never have been exposed at all.

2 Abandoned quarry

In the past, rock has been quarried on both sides of the Pass, following the steep angle of the ash beds. At each chosen level, the much prized stone was won from the mountain by burrowing caves deep underground, then carrying it to the cutting sheds on steeply inclined tramways. The supporting buttresses, where the tramway crossed the road, still make impressive portals for drivers cresting the summit.

Turn left at junction above hairpins

As you gain height, the landscape becomes more broken. Above the hairpin section of the road, large numbers of boulders perch precariously on the bare mountain rock where they were dumped by ice, providing further indications of the altitude at which ice once flowed. Signs of ice action are not, however, confined to Honister valley. As the rounded summits of the nearby fells come into view, remember that each owes its form to this part of Lakeland's history.

3 Today, quarrying for slate takes place near the summit of Fleetwith Pike in large open pits. These

pits are not safe but, when viewed from a safe vantage point, the steep slope of the shimmering grey–green slate beds can be seen. In places they are crossed by creamy-coloured sheets of rock that were formed by intense pressure when, during the ancient process of mountain building, some of the rocks were pushed past one another.

Beyond quarry make always for highest ground (track runs to right of quarry)

From the top of the quarry road you need only walk a little higher to reach the summit level of Fleetwith Pike, a marvellous vantage point for one of Lakeland's finest vistas. Stretching conspicuously away westwards from beneath the Pike

4 ✌

are the twin lakes of Buttermere and Crummock Water, each in a basin created by an ancient glacier and now being increasingly separated by the growth of a modern delta. Indeed, every small cascading fellside stream is slowly infilling the lakes as it brings pebbles, sand and clay into their still waters.

The southern margin of Buttermere is flanked by the ridge of fells running from Hay Stacks to High Style, each peak separated from the next by a great, glacially scoured hollow. This is a northeasterly facing slope, one that would have nurtured snow most easily by protecting it from the warmth of the afternoon Sun. Ice formed here first and lasted longest, and you will note that no south-facing slopes are as deeply riven as these.

Looking eastwards, let your eye range over the whole of the central Lakeland fells, each distinguished by its own shape and yet all sharing the same unifying legacy of the Ice Age. Distant Scafell and Pillar, standing conspicuously alone to the south-west of Great Gable, which rears its bulky summit to the north, all have had their sides sculptured by glaciers and chiselled by frost. Each of these mountains has resisted erosion because of its hard rocks, but their forms have been made more dramatic by eroded belts of weaker rock. For example, the defile that separates Great Gable and Green Gable has been etched by ice out of a belt of shattered rocks.

From Fleetwith Pike return to 🅿 or follow broad track towards Great Gable

In essence, the walk from Fleetwith Pike to the Gables runs across the back of the fells. The well worn path is of motorway proportions and should cause no problems. The summit of Great Gable gives the better view in really fine weather but, for those who prefer to conserve their energy, the view from Green Gable is almost as good. From Green Gable the gap separating the Gables lies below, its frost-riven and scree-littered sides now seen more

Walks 100

clearly than from Fleetwith Pike. From here, too, you can trace the line of weak shattered rocks across from the defile of Windy Gap through the saddle above Sty Head Tarn and off towards Langdale. It is an unforgettable view of glacial mountain scenery.

5 🌿

6   The giant's armchair: Harrop Tarn and Armboth Fell, Thirlmere

Introduction

You have to be feeling fairly energetic to get to the top of most of Lakeland's fells or to view its combes with their still, clear tarns. However, tucked out of the way, on the far side of Thirlmere, the North West Water Authority has obligingly provided a route to one of the prettiest of all tarns, and an extension on to the fell by using gentle paths. From the top you can see Helvellyn away to the east, and peaks of Great Gable and Scafell to the south-west.

➔ Harrop Tarn
🅿 is 1 mile (1.6 km) from south end of Thirlmere. From Ambleside, A591 [Keswick >] then left [Armboth >] after Dunmail Raise. From Keswick, A591 [Ambleside >] then right [Thirlmere >] before lake

The walks

In both these walks the steepest section is at the start and takes about half an hour.

(a) Short and moderately easy with steps. Follow **1,2,3** and return (1½ hours).

(b) Longer, mostly on gently sloping forest tracks, and with superb views at the end. Follow **1,2, 3,4** and return (half a day).

The route

1 Follow green posts from corner of 🅿

When Manchester Corporation obtained permission to build a dam at the northern end of Thirlmere and to enlarge the lake to its present size, they were only taking advantage of the work of a large ice tongue. Thousands of years before, this tongue of ice had scoured out a huge irregular trench to replace the small valley of the Wyth Burn.

Thirlmere valley is a clear illustration of a glaciated valley with a U-shaped profile. It sweeps down from Helvellyn in the east and up again to Ullscarf in the west. The glacier scoured not only deeply downwards but also sideways until the valley was sufficiently straightened to allow the easy passage of an almost rigid ice stream. Although the main source of the ice was to the south of where you now stand, tributary glaciers emerged from the headwater hollows of former streams high up on the fellsides. One of these was Dob Gill, whose ice slowly scoured its headwater

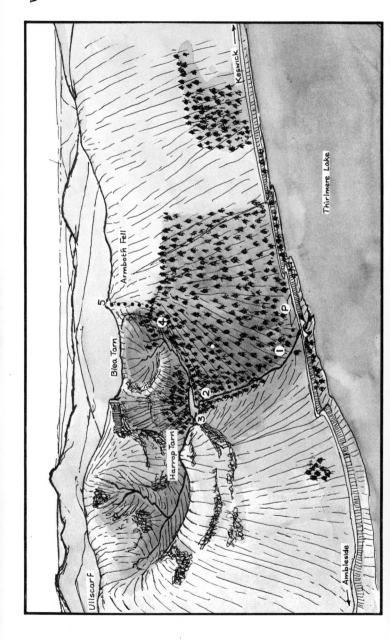

valley into the beautiful hollow we are now to visit. But these small glaciers could never match the depth of erosion achieved by the main valley ice stream, so our route must first climb the steep valley side.

As you climb the forested slopes, notice that the trail is strewn with partly rounded boulders. These are the tools of the valley glacier, the mammoth-sized pieces of scouring powder torn from rocks further up the valley, scraped along for a while, and then abandoned when the ice melted.

2   The main rocks of the area are of volcanic origin, layers of lavas and ashes long ago compacted into really hard materials. However, within them are some less resistant layers and, as the path becomes less steep, you begin to hear the consequences of these variations. Following your ears rather than your eyes will soon take you to the left of the path towards a magnificent waterfall whose white foaming waters mark the boundary between the valley and tarn. Large boulders lie where the ice dumped them some 12 000 years ago. Because the rocks at the top of the waterfall are tougher than those below, first ice and later the river have been able to carry away the weaker rocks and sharpen the waterfall crest.

3   Above the waterfall, the valley is gentler, and a pleasant stroll through the forest soon brings you to a delightful view of Harrop Tarn. Here, in the morning, photographers can capture Ullscarf mirrored by the lake, in a rare scene of tranquillity. There is a footpath around most of the lake, although in places it is rather spongy underfoot. Nevertheless, it is worth following, because you can see how the small streams are slowly filling in the tarn with silt brought off the fell, and how the tarn occupies a bowl shaped hollow whose steep 'back wall' contrasts with its more gentle sides.

From Harrop Tarn follow white markers. Where forest road reaches its highest point, take footpath up hill through forest out on to fell

From the path at the foot of the back wall you can now see Helvellyn rising above the trees. If you want a more extensive view, follow the white trail posts up round the tarn and towards Armboth Fell.

Where the foresters have cut drainage ditches either side of the road, you can glimpse the typical chaos of boulders and clays that have been left behind as further reminders of the Ice Age.

4   Just before the forest ends, the path becomes more gentle again and, emerging from the trees out on to the fell, you will find yourself on the broad back of the open mountain. By progressing only a short distance further, you will be rewarded with a

Harrop Tarn and Armboth Fell, Thirlmere   103

panorama. Any of the local summits will do, but with a little extra effort you can go to the highest point and look down over Blea Tarn.

Blea Tarn is quite a contrast to Harrop Tarn; no steep back walls here, just gentle slopes down to the water's edge. Possibly the ice never became thick enough to erode a deep hollow, or perhaps the rock is just too hard. Whatever the reason, it is nevertheless a true glacially sculptured hollow, sitting high on the fell. Beyond it, the land drops away to the picturesque valley of Watendlath and Derwentwater, whose secrets may tempt you to try Walk 3.

Return to 🅿 following white markers

7 Steps in the valley: Aira Force

Introduction

Among the most attractive of Lakeland's natural features are its waterfalls. Sometimes, in dry weather, these are no more than silken threads delicately tracing a path down the valley side. Occasionally, after a storm, they are raging torrents of muddy brown cascading water. Almost all the waterfalls are, like the lakes, an indirect result of glacial activity, largely because some glaciers could scour deeper than others. In general, the biggest glaciers carved the largest and deepest valleys. For example, the glacier that spilled from the hollows on Helvellyn's flanks carved the valley in which Ullswater now lies. However, not all ice streams were as large or able to achieve such massive scouring as the trunk glaciers; many tributary valleys were therefore left hanging high above the main valley floors. As the ice melted away and rivers replaced glaciers, the differences in valley floor height could be overcome only by cascades and waterfalls. Aira Force and neighbouring High Force are the most dramatic of a 'flight' of waterfalls that allow water to tumble from the hanging valley of Matterdale down to the valley floor of Ullswater. Both waterfalls are pleasing at any time, but they are at their most dramatic just after a period of rainy weather.

🚗 from Keswick, A66 [Penrith >], right A5091 [Matterdale >]. 🅿 as soon as you see Ullswater. From Ambleside, [Windermere >] then left onto A592 [Penrith >]. Aira Force is just beyond junction with A5091 [Matterdale >] 🅿 (or 🅿 on Matterdale road above falls)

The walks

(a) Short and quite easy (Aira Force only). Follow **5,4,3** and start at lakeside car park (about 1 hour).

(b) Longer, higher but still mainly on well made tracks. Follow **1,2,3,4** and return (about 2½ hours).

(c) Superb views over Ullswater without any steep paths. Follow **1,2,3,4,6,5** and return.

(Opposite) **As water spills from Harrop Tarn down the mountainside to Thirlmere it forms a waterfall**

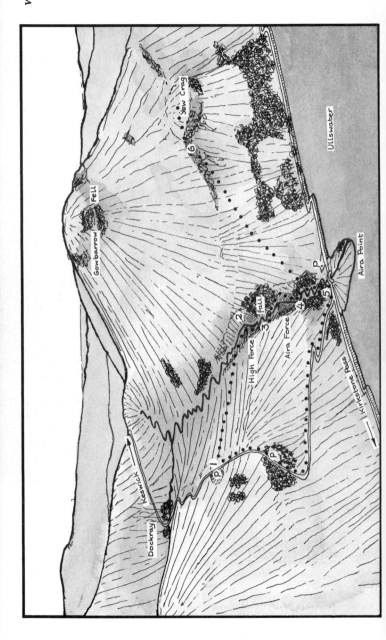

Keswick

Dockray

Gowbarrow Fell

Sew Crag

6

High Force

Aira Force

Fall

2

3

4

5

P

P

P

Aira Point

Kirkstone Pass

Ullswater

High Force

The route

1 From **P** near Dockray enter 'Gowbarrow' (NT) and walk to stream

The floor of the hanging valley near Dockray provides one of the best places from which to see how different were the erosive effects of large and small glaciers. Here, the valley is wide and shallow, its steep, craggy sides the main evidence that a glacier once passed this way. There is really no sign that the valley is shortly to end in the steep wall of the Ullswater vale.

Although initially you will be oblivious to the change in slope just a little further on, you gain

quite a different impression as soon as you reach
2 Aira Beck, set in its narrow ribbon of woodland.
Here, High Force, the upper of the two major
waterfalls, cascades over a vertical wall of tough
volcanic rock, plunges into a deep, almost circular
pool and finally passes through a narrow cleft in a
further rock band. Here is clear evidence that Aira
Beck is cutting its valley headwards and is being
temporarily frustrated by tougher rock bands
standing vertically across its path.

Below High Force the valley becomes wider as a
3 much less resistant belt of rocks is crossed. Here,
the river simply cascades and tumbles over small
rapids, but suddenly the beck again plunges over a
vertical face and disappears into a deep, dark
gorge. This is an interesting fall because, the more
you look at it, the more it becomes clear that its
shape is largely caused by the hand of man. The
defile is some 20 ft (6 m) deep and a very regular
6 ft (1.8 m) wide, a regularity that is quite unlike the
work of Nature. The trench carries on beyond the
waterfall, confirming that this is really an old mine,
once worked while the stream was diverted but
now used by the stream.

There is a small wooden bridge spanning the
downstream end of the artificial trench, from which
you can look back along the defile. The view down
stream is even more spectacular, for here the beck
has cut a more winding, natural gorge, providing
considerable evidence of fluctuation of stream level
and the manner of water erosion. Notice how the
banks are clear of algae, and how the highest level
of clean rock is a good 3 ft (1 m) above summer low
water. In the stream bed are circular holes drilled by
pebbles as they are swirled around by water, not
perhaps under the placid conditions in which you
may see the stream, but under the flood conditions
of winter.

4   Below this gorge the valley opens out once more
and the river flows quietly and smoothly as though
it were in a low-lying valley, even though we are
still above the main drop to Ullswater – the typical
form of a hanging valley. Then, as you descend,
quite suddenly a little stone bridge comes into
view, often crowded with people. As soon as
you reach the bridge the reason for the crowd's
presence will be clear: the bridge has been built just
at the point where the beck plummets more than
60 ft (18 m) as the famous waterfall of Aira Force.

(Opposite) **Aira Force during dry weather**

Aira Force is best seen from below, where the lower bridge provides a marvellous view towards the sparkling waters as they shoot over the rock lip below the top bridge before plunging to the valley. Notice the similarities between Aira Force and High Force: both have cut narrow clefts in the valley and are slowly cutting their way even further up stream; and both have succeeded in breaking through one tough rock band and are presently attacking another.

At the foot of Aira Force you are almost at the level of Ullswater. Three huge leaps and a mile of cascades have brought the stream down some 300 ft (91 m) to where it now flows casually along its last journey to the lake. Its decreased speed means that the stream cannot carry its load of silt, clay and pebbles, which are therefore discarded to form the delta of Aira Point.

The shore at Aira Point makes a good picnic – or resting-place before you return along the Matterdale road to the car park, or venture further along the edge of Gowbarrow Fell to above Yew Crag and the Memorial Seat.

The walk down past the falls has been in the shady seclusion of a narrow strip of forest. However, the track across the lower slopes of Gowbarrow Fell is across open grassland, and this gives an opportunity to get some of the best views of Ullswater and the high fells. As the track makes its way across the fellside and above the forests, the wide, open form of the valley, which has been shaped by ice, becomes clear. Ullswater merely fills up the bottom of an enormous rocky trench over 1000 ft (305 m) deep when measured from the top of Gowbarrow Fell, or over 1100 ft (335 m) from the summit of High Dodd on the opposite shore. This is glacial erosion on a grand scale and it is best seen from the Memorial Seat. Here, you can look northwards to the subdued and rounded fells that have been carved in relatively weak rocks. Then turn round and look south, to the grandeur of the tough central fells, their volcanic rocks culminating in the ridge of Helvellyn (3116 ft; 950 m) off to the right. Whereas the ice-scoured valley is wide and open to the north, it is steep and narrow as it enters the high fells, confining Ullswater into a narrow ribbon of shimmering water set amongst an impressive cluster of peaks. The nearest fell on the far bank is Silver Crag, which rises to the dumpy top of Birk Fell (1670 ft; 509 m). Directly opposite, and on the right of the lake, is the nearer fell of Glenridding

5 Aira Point
🚻 WC 🅿

Broad path leads
across open fell
from gate up stream
of car park

6

Dodd. Although this is a mere 1343 ft (409 m) it is completely dwarfed, first by Sheffield Pike (2215 ft; 675 m) and then by the even higher fell of St Sunday Crag (2756 ft; 840 m) on the skyline. Finally, the broad ridge in the distance and directly beyond the lake is the mass of Fairfield (2863 ft; 873 m) and its neighbouring Hart Crag (2698 ft; 822 m). No wonder this is one of Lakeland's most famous views.

8 Beneath England's highest street: Hayeswater

Introduction
Have you ever wished you could get in among the high fells instead of just driving past them, without needing outstanding physical fitness and climbing gear? One way, described in Walk 5, is to leave the road as it crests a pass and then to follow the ridge tops. This is possible in the western fells but there are no really convenient passes in the east. Another approach, therefore, is to walk along the floor of a valley that eventually leads to a relatively easy path on to the high fells. One of the most charming places for such a valley walk is near the southern end of Ullswater, in the heart of the eastern fells and beneath the old Roman routeway of High Street.

The walks

🚗 from Windermere, [Ambleside >], then A592 [Penrith >]. After Brothers Water right [Hartsop >]. 🅿 beyond hamlet

(a) Short and easy to see the ice-formed valley before Hayeswater. Follow **1,2** and return (45 minutes).

(b) The shortest route to Hayeswater runs along a well made track of moderate gradient. Follow **1,2,3** and return (3 hours).

(c) To include a pleasant walk round the lake. Follow **1,2,3,4,5,3** and return (4 hours).

(d) For the more energetic, to include High Street. Follow **1,2,3,6,4,5,3** and return. Carry waterproofs, guard against cool air on the fell-top. The walk takes most of a day: take your sandwiches. Take heed of the local weather forecast.

The route
The eastern fells consist of a number of radiating ridges to the east of Kirkstone Pass, each leading away from the 2000+ ft (614+ m) ridge that connects the Knott to High Street. During the Ice Age, the deep hollows on the flanks of this central region saw snow slowly turn to ice, which flowed outwards along old river valleys in the direction of Ullswater in the west and Haweswater in the east. Although these were powerful individual streams of ice, each alone could not achieve the spectacular rate of scouring possible when all the flows were

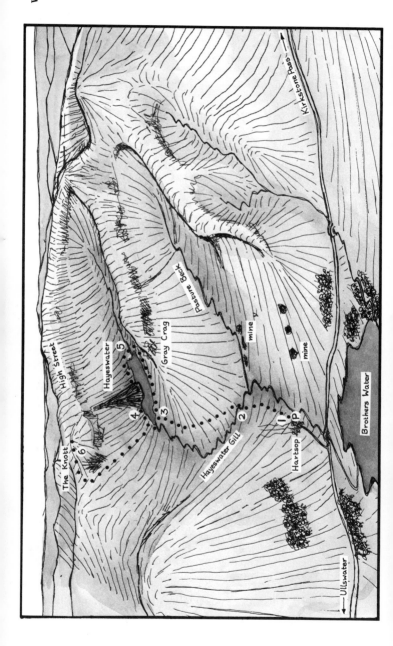

The Knott
High Street
Hayeswater
6
5
4
3
Gray Crag
Pasture Beck
Hayeswater Gill
2
1
P
Hartsop
mine
mine
Brothers Water
Kirkstone Pass
Ullswater

combined. Consequently, valleys can be seen to widen and deepen conspicuously below the junction of every pair of valleys. Such contrasts are especially noticeable where all the eastern ice streams merged with those from the flanks of Helvellyn to form the massive trunk glacier that excavated the dale in which Ullswater now lies.

The route you are about to follow up to Hayeswater from the main valley consists of a number of distinct steps: first, a 'riser' to the area of Hartsop car park; then a level 'tread' to the confluence of the Hayeswater Gill and the Pasture Beck; then one more 'riser' up to the level of Hayeswater. Beyond each step the valley narrows slightly; the valley at Hayeswater is only two-thirds of its width lower down at Hartsop.

1 🅿 Hayeswater   Hartsop is one of the truly remote farming hamlets of Lakeland. Like Watendlath in Borrowdale (Walk 3), its few cottages of rough-hewn volcanic stone huddle together on one side of the valley, away from winter floods and at the limit of improved farmland. Beyond lies the wild upland of the eastern fells, a steep land of bold crags that defy the hand of even the most fervent farmer. Today it is mainly tourists who tread the broad, stony track to Hayeswater, which otherwise is left to the hardy sheep.

As soon as you leave the car park, the overwhelming impression is of a landscape fashioned entirely by the relentless hand of ice erosion. Ahead lies the wide sweep of the classic U-shaped valley, its steep upper slopes rugged and sharp, deeply etched not just by ice but also by frost shattering. Now littered with this frost-riven debris, which has fallen from the crags, the lower valley flanks are less steep, their covering of grass and bracken softening the sharp blocky scree.

Although erosion has been dominant here, the hummocky terrain near the car park is formed of piles of boulder clay dumped by the ice as it finally melted away. Man has added to this scene, as well as Nature, for some of the piles of material are of rock-spoil from old mines. In this area, spoil heaps still pick out the direction of a vein of rich ore laid bare by ice erosion but now long since worked out.

Hartsop lies in the broad valley below the junction of two smaller valleys sweeping down from
2 High Street. At the bridge near the stream junction, the grandeur of the first of these valleys comes fully into view. Its headwaters are guarded by the peaks of Stoney Cove Pike and Thornthwaite Crag.

An old 'slate'-built house in Hartsop: its upper floor was once used as a spinning gallery

Nearby are shafts and tunnels and the remains of a huge waterwheel, which powered a crushing hammer. Despite having been abandoned less than a hundred years ago, few discernible pieces of the mine remain, apart from the small spoil heaps and the trough that housed the wheel. As if to highlight the way Nature reclaims her own, a small tree now sprouts in the wheel pit, protected from grazing at its sapling stage by the man-made stone-work.

Above the bridge you enter Hayeswater dale and begin the steeper ascent up one of the 'risers'. Thus, while you maintain an even grade cut into the hillside by man, the river tumbles and falls continually. This steep section of path tends to focus the eyes on the track rather than on the land-scape, but even here there are points of interest. Laid across the track are modern V-shaped struc-tures of concrete. These are arranged to channel water from the path into a drain, to prevent further erosion where countless feet have worn away the natural vegetation and trampled the earth, thereby encouraging water to run over the surface rather than to sink in.

On the right, the broad convex slope leading up to Gray Crag throws off the water and is devoid of surface streams. On the left, the concave slopes below Rest Dodd curve inwards to collect surface water into several tiny streams. Although these streams tumble over the rocks as they pick at the scree-mantled hillside, as yet they have made little impression on the solid rock beneath.

Here, Hayeswater Gill occupies a steep ravine and the path skirts the side of Gray Crag, gradually gaining in height as the valley gets wider. Soon there is the first sight of the background ridge of High Street. Nevertheless, the lake itself remains hidden from view until the very last moment for, although the path eventually flattens considerably and the whole ice-scoured mountain hollow is clearly revealed, Hayeswater is shielded behind an artificial concrete dam.

3   From the dam you can look out over nearly a mile of clear blue lake. If the water outflow is small enough, you can stand on the dam, bend down to water level and get a fish's-eye view of the splendid sweeping curves of this remote Lakeland valley. Whether it be from the waterline or from near the bridge, you have to be impressed by the line of ice-sculptured precipices that sweep from the Knott along the flanks of High Street. Below the steepest

Beside Hayeswater, showing mounds of glacial moraine near the far lake shore.

slopes, fans of scree give a ruffled appearance to the hillsides.

Try to imagine the huge amount of rock removed to produce this impressive amphitheatre, then linger for a while by the dam to see more detail. At first, the fell slopes appear to curve down and under the lake, but notice how the lakeside is really dominated by hummocks. Begin to walk round the lake shore and you will find the path rising and falling, twisting and turning. Look across the lake and you will see that the hummocks occur along the valley length, their irregular forms probably more or less as they were left as dumps of boulder clay by the last remains of the Hayeswater glacier.

The lakeside walk reveals yet more points of detail. Ahead lies a large fan of rock debris swept from the fellsides and now pushing ever further into the lake. The mantle of light green (more fertile) grass distinguishes its outlines from the yellow–brown colour of the other mountain grasses, a sign of how the landscape is slowly changing. There are also other signs: the hummocks of boulder clay are already being trimmed by lapping waves on the lake, causing their softer material to collapse.

As the head of the valley comes into view, the extent of the ice-dumped rock waste is very clear, for it litters the valley bottom. As yet, the stream flowing into Hayeswater has managed to cut little more than a ravine into the hillocks of debris, but every fragment it manages to move is used to build a delta out into the head of the lake. There is certainly no lack of material waiting to be transferred from the valley head and, as you walk past it, you see a barren part of Lakeland looking much as it did soon after the glaciers had disappeared.

Hayeswater is superb when seen from the lakeside; if you have enough energy, it becomes spectacular when viewed from the ridge of High Street. The ridge is really a place for fell-walkers, although it can be briefly sampled by a short 'walk' up to the Knott. From the summit the whole plan of the ice-sculptured valley is laid out as if on a map: the U-shaped profile; the steep frost-riven cliffs near the top; the piles of hummocky boulder clay in the bottom. You can also look down into the lake through its clear waters and see how fingers of the deltas are pushing slowly forwards. If you climb High Street, take a map with you to identify the fells and lakes stretching away in all directions. For example, you can see the elusive summit of Helvellyn directly to the west, and the shimmering ribbon of Ullswater. As you admire the view, you can reflect on the fact that this was the view seen by the Romans when they toiled to engineer England's highest street.

9   The lake of swans: Elterwater

Introduction
The low-lying land around Elterwater does not fit neatly into the scheme of valleys that characterise much of the central Lake District. In this enclave of lowland there is an opportunity to wander peacefully in gentle scenery, much of it forested, and always with a background of distant fells. The route is mainly over flat land, along paths meandering beneath the shade of trees and beside lakes or swift streams. Because many of the views are of nearby features, this walk is not likely to be marred by low cloud.

🚗 from Ambleside, A593 [Coniston >]. In 3 miles (5 km) at Skelwith Bridge turn right B5343 [Langdale >]. 🅿 ½ mile (0.8 km) right in NT quarry (Seathwaite)

The walks
(a) Short and easy. Follow **1,2,3,4,7,8** (2½ hours).
(b) Longer and easy. Follow **1** through to **8** (half a day).

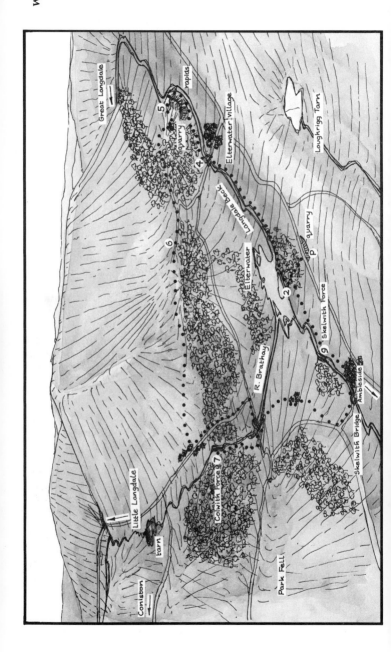

Great Longdale

rapids

5

quarry

Elterwater village

Little Longdale

tarn

Coniston

6

Langdale Beck

Elterwater

R. Brathay

Colwith Force 7

Park Fell

Loughrigg Tarn

quarry

2

Skelwith Force

9

Skelwith Bridge

Ambleside

The route

1 Cross road and proceed to lake shore, follow right

Seathwaite car park is the floor of a disused quarry in the walls of which you can look at the grey–green rock found throughout central Lakeland. Sometimes, dark green pinhead-sized blotches seem as though they have been splashed on the rock, showing where gas bubbles of an ancient lava have since been filled up with minerals. Elsewhere, the rock is fine-grained, representing old ash beds. Whether they are derived from ash or from lava, the rocks have remained very resistant to erosion by water and ice. They underlie all the route, sometimes rising to the surface as rocky knobs standing proud of the flat land, elsewhere hidden by a veneer of soil or boulder clay and revealed only where streams have carried the overlying debris away.

2   On the further lake shore the flat land has now been colonised by rushes, and even trees have begun to grow. All the flat land beside Elterwater, a sombre lake set among the peaks of Langdale, was once part of the lake bed. Lakes do not last long, especially small saucer-shaped hollows in the floor of a glacially scoured upland, and nearby Rydal Water is already almost filled in. With the cascading streams of Langdale Beck entering from the west and the River Brathay from the south, there is no shortage of sediment.

Between the still lake waters and Elterwater
3   village Great Langdale Beck flows briskly. Through its clear waters shines a bed of pebbles, the final remnants of the boulder clay left behind by the glaciers. The finest material has long ago been washed onwards to start filling in the lake. Now it is being joined more slowly by the pebbles that bounce just a little further down stream with each winter storm.

Rivers always follow winding courses, and as the water follows each bend it is thrown outwards where it undercuts the outer bank. This motion leaves slack water on the inside bends. Here banks of pebbles have built up. By continually eroding one bank and depositing on the other, rivers keep their channels the same width even though they change course. This changing course can present problems to the path-makers. In an attempt to stop the shift of the river, they have dumped large rocks where the water erodes most strongly. It will be interesting to see whether they have succeeded in halting Nature.

From time immemorial, people have had to come to terms with rivers. Bridge-builders in particular

4 At Elterwater
village cross bridge
and follow up stream
on left bank.
Elterwater 🍴 ☎
🚻 **WC**

have had to face the problem of shifting river
channels. The choice of a bridge site at Elterwater
village was not at all haphazard, for the old bridge
engineers could not build on the lake peats
and were faced with an additional problem, the
presence of a deep gorge slightly up stream. As you
stand on the village bridge, you can see that their
solution was as practical as the bridge is elegant.
They built the bridge on the last patch of solid rock
just as the gorge gives way to the peaty lake muds.
Beside this strategic crossing point the village grew,
possibly over a thousand years ago. More recently,
when industry came to Lakeland, the gorge that for
so long had been a disadvantage became a major
bonus for the villagers. To the right of the bridge
(looking up stream) is a deep stone trough, the last
remnant of a waterwheel used to power a gun-
powder works that once supplied many Lakeland
mines and quarries.

Almost everything in Elterwater village has
changed since earlier years. The riverside cottages,
for example, have been converted in such a way
that their earlier industrial functions are now quite
undetectable.

At the bridge, solid rock appears in the landscape
for the first time since the car-park quarry. It is still
greenish grey in colour, but is now angled steeply
into the river bed, each layer of rock tipped on edge
and exposed to the scouring action of the river.
Notice how the bouncing pebbles have sculptured
the rock, drilling holes and turning the river bed
into an egg box of pinnacles and hollows. You will
be able to see a rounded hollow, still with its
eroding pebbles inside, ready to drill further into
the rock with the next storm flow.

5   Beyond the bridge you are in quarry country.
Above the river rise huge heaps of rock discarded
from the quarry higher on the hill. Nowadays, rock
is quarried by blasting from the faces of huge pits,
but in earlier times horizontal tunnels (adits) were
used. They can still be seen in the hillside beside the
quarry road, but do not enter them, as they are
unstable and liable to collapse.

Follow track up hill
through quarry yard

Elterwater quarries produce some of the famous
Cumberland stone that is shipped all over the
world to face buildings, make fireplaces, grace
graveyards and make bases for ornaments. However, much of the 'slate' you see in the quarry
yard is no more a true slate than are most other
Cumbrian rocks given that name. It is a beautiful
green rock made from fragments of volcanic ash

Walks 120

that have become welded together. The name 'slate', in this context, simply means that the rock will split or can be cut into thin sheets. As you follow the footpath round beneath the quarry spoil heap, then up the hill between two huge walls of waste stone and into the quarry yard, you can see some of the enormous variety of cut slabs, a few of which are displayed in the showroom.

From the far side of the quarry there is a clear view up Langdale to the prominent crags of the Langdale Pikes. However, nearer at hand you can also see the enormous spoil heaps and you may wonder why the material cannot be used or dumped more efficiently.

At lodge house go straight up hill through woods following track between 2 low walls on right of spoil heap. At road beyond, turn right then left through kissing-gate. Go across the field bearing left. Go through gap in far wall

The hill above the quarry is heavily wooded, although not so densely as to obscure the view of even older spoil heaps, but it is a walk more for views than for scenery. When finally you emerge from the woods into open country, the fells re-appear, this time as a backdrop to Little Langdale and yet more quarries. Below is the River Brathay, meandering over a flat tract of country. Tucked away in the folds of the valley lies the small lake of Little Langdale Tarn, which, just like Elterwater, is impounded by a particularly resistant band of glacially smoothed rock. You get a feeling that changes are at hand as you leave the scattered cottages of Little Langdale village. First, the hills

Little Langdale ⊕ (on right along road). Turn left at road

begin closing in about you; then, forest clothes both slopes and the road rises high above the river, which remains detectable only as a rushing sound below. This is not the quiet Brathay of the village area, but a swift river about to cascade over a rock bar to form the famous waterfalls of Colwith Force. (Colwith is derived from the Viking 'place in the forest where charcoal was burned' and 'force', meaning waterfall, is also of Viking derivation, from 'fors'.)

Colwith Force rushes over a rock step that withstood even the power of the Lakeland glaciers. It is also a potential source of power for mills and for metal-working. The forest of coppiced woodland oak, ash, alder, birch and willow (all cut for charcoal before the discovery of coke smelting) still surrounds the falls. Wherever you see coppiced wood it is a sure sign that metal-working was once carried on nearby. Today, the National Trust maintains both woods and waterfall in as natural a state as possible so that the waters of the Brathay may tumble down over the last rocks before being lost in the quiet stillness of Elterwater.

6 At road junction turn right. On right [Colwith Force >]. Opposite path [Skelwith Bridge >] (follow past one farm then through yard of second farm along track bearing right)

In its last few hundred yards the Brathay flows gently over alluvium – fine sand, silt and clay washed from the boulder clays of the upper valley and now dumped abruptly along what was once the lake shore. The river has not quite lost all of its energy and it swings hard up against the rock on which our footpath runs, undercutting the soil and revealing the roots of trees penetrating deep into cracks in the rock. Only because they have such firm anchorage can the trees avoid tumbling headlong into the water.

8 Skelwith Bridge 🅿
WC ♿ **M** Over bridge turn left through slate works [Skelwith Force >]

Skelwith Bridge has a site almost identical to that of Elterwater, and, like the latter, is famous for its quarry (again volcanic ash) and its waterfall. Search carefully beside the waterfall and, just as with Elterwater, you will see signs of old millraces – the last vestige of a once-important rural industry.

Skelwith Force, as it cascades over the rock bar that holds up the lake, is a fitting dramatic climax to the Elterwater walk. Because it is made of tough ash, even the foaming waters of the Brathay seem unable to make much impact on this massive rock. Beyond lie the still waters of the lake.

10   In sight of the pikes: Blea Tarn, Little Langdale

Introduction

Great Langdale and Little Langdale are corridors of lowland among the high peaks of the central fells. They are roughly parallel valleys, striking westwards from their confluence at Elterwater and separated by the broad bulk of Lingmoor and Wrymore Fells. Although the intervening fell is wide for most of its length, in the centre a deep 'bite' has been taken out of it, narrowing it by some two-thirds. In the middle of this 'bite' lies Blea Tarn, a pretty stretch of water not far from some of Lakeland's most celebrated pikes (peaks).

🚗 from Ambleside, A593 [Coniston >]. At Skelwith Bridge [Great Langdale B5343 >] to valley end. 🅿 1 mile (1.6 km) beyond summit crest opposite Blea Tarn

The walks
(a) Short and easy around the tarn. Follow **1,3,4** (1½ hours).
(b) Longer, still without steep slopes, and with views to the distant fells. Follow **1** through to **5** (half a day).

The route
Walking is the best way to enter a Lakeland valley. This is certainly the case with the little valley con-

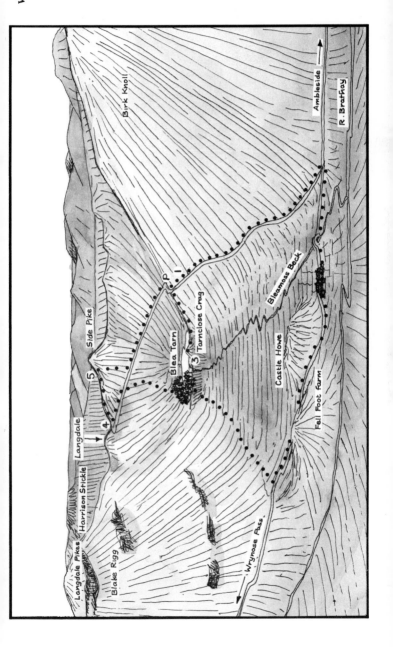

Langdale Pikes • Harrison Stickle • Side Pike • Birk Knoll • Blake Rigg • Langdale • Blea Tarn • Tarnclose Crag • Wrynose Pass • Castle Howe • Bleamoss Beck • Fell Foot farm • Ambleside • R. Brathay

taining Blea Tarn, for then you can see the grandeur of the fells grouped around its head. However, the restricted local parking makes a short walk necessary, but this is of considerable interest, for it gives sweeping views over Little Langdale, a wide, flat-floored glaciated valley.

The road into Little Langdale has been engineered to cling tightly to the valley side, thereby avoiding the wetter lowland, until it joins the road from Wrynose Pass. This, too, clings to the higher (and drier) ground for as long as possible, and follows the dale bottom for only a short distance.

The road provides excellent vantage points from which to see how farming has survived in this difficult landscape. Notice how Fell Foot farm below in the valley is built firmly on a ledge of land free from floods. Although apparently exposed to all the elements, the site is actually well sheltered from harsh winds from Wrynose in the west by the knob of upstanding rock called Castle Howe, and the buildings are set end-on as protection against any severe weather from the pass above Blea Tarn. High stone walls and a scattering of trees complete its defences. However, there is no defence from the rain and frequent cloud, which together help to create poor grazing land. Near the farm buildings, grasslands have been improved to allow better overwintering of stock. The stone walls testify to many years of painstaking clearance of glacial rubble from the fields, but beyond these small enclosures the fells remain as wild and barren as ever.

The valley linking the two Langdales is mainly the product of glacial erosion. As you look up to it from the road, its open U shape hangs above Little Langdale and tells of an ice stream less powerful than the one that carved the trunk valley now followed by the Brathay river.

As Bleamoss Beck, the stream draining Blea Tarn, tumbles and splashes in a gorge gashed through Tarnclose Crag, it falls over a rock bar – a band of tough volcanic rock straddling the valley of which the crag is the highest remnant. On the fellside to the right, the same rock builds the crags of Birk Knott, and to the left are further small crags running up to Blake Rigg.

Once you are at the top of Tarnclose Crag, you will find that it is not only a splendid panoramic

1

2 Just beyond Castle Howe rock, cross the valley aiming for the ledge of higher ground to left of the peat bog (it *is* a public footpath)

viewpoint, but also a place where ice has clearly
3 scratched at the bare rock surface facing the tarn
and plucked great blocks from the side facing Little
Langdale. To do this, the ice must have come
towards you from 'up stream', yet beyond the tarn
there is no valley head to be seen, no high, fellside
hollow in which snow could have gathered to form
into glacier ice. Instead there is a low saddle, now
used by the only road to connect the Langdales. If
you had been able to visit this valley before the Ice
Age, you would have found a high unbroken ridge
stretching round from Brown Howe to Blake Rigg.
During the Ice Age, however, Great Langdale must
have become so choked with ice that it overflowed,
some of it southwards into Little Langdale, lower-
ing the saddle to the form you see today and
leaving only Side Pike as a reminder of a once
unbroken mountain ridge.

4 ❧   From the saddle beside the road a wonderful
panorama of central Lakeland comes into view.
Ahead is the tent-shaped top of Harrison Stickle
(Stickle is derived from the Viking word meaning
'sharp peak'). To its left stands the peak of Pike
O'Stickle. Together these two peaks are known as
the Langdale Pikes. Below stretches the Great
Langdale valley, one of Lakeland's finest glacial
troughs with its two tributaries of Oxendale (left)
and Mickleden (ahead).

At the head of Mickleden a sharply defined notch
cuts the skyline. This notch and Angle Tarn
(beyond) at the head of the Seathwaite valley
(Walk 4) complete a tract of shattered rocks that
have been etched out by glacial erosion along a
line beginning with Windy Gap near Great Gable
(Walk 5) and making an extraordinary high-level
pass in otherwise impenetrable fells.

Between the head of Mickleden and the Langdale
Pikes, another notch, known as Stake Pass, marks
the pack-horse road that linked Langdale to
Barrowdale.

In Langdale itself, the boulder clay, left after
the glaciers finally melted, is under attack by the
Langdale Beck, leaving only a multitude of larger
boulders strewn across its floor.

The Oxendale Beck in particular is very prone to
flooding, because it is the 'spout' of a funnel-
shaped range of mountains. There have been many
attempts to control this wild stream, as the concrete
barriers across its path indicate. Valley dwellers
have avoided the stream and built their houses on
drier land on the sunny side of the valley. Here,

Follow lakeside track up to road. Over stile beside cattle grid then towards Side Pike

too, the boulder clay has remained protected from the rivers and it forms the basis for the poor soil.

Side Pike is the culmination of the route around Blea Tarn and from its summit the bowl shape of the valley containing the lake is exceptionally clear. Beyond it, Tarnclose Crag stands proudly before softer rock is reached and the valley floor falls

5 ⚘ steeply to Little Langdale below. It is also from here, looking down at the tiny sheet of shimmering water set within the valley floor, that we can appreciate how much larger the lake must once have been. Those reedy lake edges that you walked beside earlier, and the peaty land between you and the lake, show the size of the earlier, much larger lake before the present streams began to fill it with silt, sand and clay from the fellsides.

11   The iron road: Boot Fell

Introduction

Boot (derived from the Viking word for a dwelling place) is a small group of granite houses firmly embedded in a fold of the hillside where an ancient trackway crosses Eskdale fell to Wasdale in the west. Everything about Boot is granite: it huddles about a stream that cascades over rounded granite rocks; it is overshadowed by the lumpy granite fells; and it is trapped within a maze of rounded granite boulders once transported by an ice sheet and since laboriously removed from the fields and piled into thick dry-stone walls by farmers.

There must once have been many boulders on the soil surface near Boot, because the field walls are sometimes over 6 ft (1.8 m) high, often nearly as thick as they are tall. Notice the small fields, a striking indication of the hard struggle to reclaim every fragment of land and of the multitude of stones to be moved. Today, sheep graze in fields without a stone in sight, but try to imagine the contents of the walls scattered on the fields and you will appreciate what has been achieved. If you find this difficult to visualise, look up to the fells around and imagine clearing the boulders you see there, for this is what the farmlands of Boot once looked like. Indeed the vanished glaciers still influence most of the life of Boot. The steep course of the Willan Beck, as it tumbles down the bottom of its valley to meet the glacially deepened Esk, owes its waterfall – and source of power for the corn mill – to glacial scouring; boulder clay provides the basis of the farmland; and the same erosive action has exposed bare rock for the miner and the quarryman to exploit.

The cottages of Boot were built with the boulders picked from the fields, as the rounded shapes of the wall stones indicate. The gaps are filled with smaller pieces of rubble, and then the whole outside surface given a waterproof mortar face. Further afield, granite was in demand for much grander buildings as well as for road surfaces, so the fells eventually became prey to the quarryman. Nevertheless, for

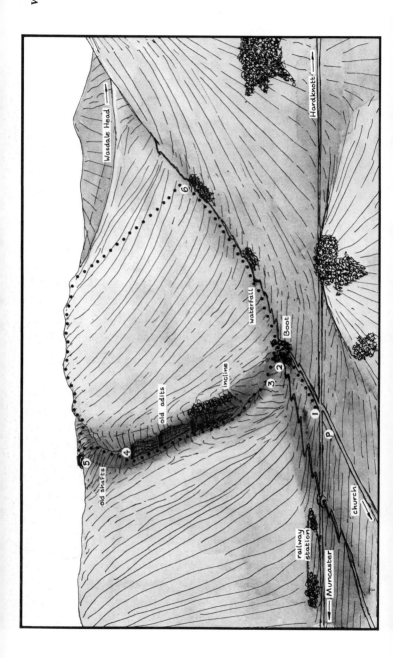

Wasdale Head

old shafts

railway station

Muncaster

old adits

incline

waterfall

Boot

church

Hardknott

Daffodils along the rough granite track that leads from Boot (2) up across the fell

the most part, the quarries are not conspicuous in the landscape today.

The most dramatic part of Boot's history can hardly be seen at all. To find it, you need to look up at the fell behind the cottages. At first it appears to be a very ordinary hillside mixture of short grasses overlying granite, meandering dry-stone walls and the occasional ruined building that looks like an old deserted barn. But there *is* something very strange about this hill. Almost directly above the houses, the post office and the inn, a deep red wound scars the fellside – a gash that begins right on the valley floor and etches its way upwards ending in a notch in the skyline. This is where a prospector first discovered one of the richest veins of iron in Lakeland.

Imagine the scene some 130 years ago when this remote and close-knit farming hamlet was overwhelmed by an army of 300 miners, who lived in rough wooden shacks near the foot of the mine. At the foot of the workings a crude railway was constructed, along which horse-drawn wagons carried the iron ore the few hundred yards to the new steam railway whence it was swiftly carried to the voracious Barrow iron furnaces.

Iron ore was discovered late at Boot: hundreds of years after the first copper mines near Keswick and nearly 2000 years after the mines of the Romans. The discovery was an important prize, a collection of veins of nearly pure iron that dipped steeply into the hillside. It was a Lakeland miniature of the internationally famous Kiruna iron seam in Sweden, in effect a lens-shaped block of iron standing on edge and exposed along one side by glacial erosion. A miniature it certainly was: often less than 1 yd (1 m) wide, it took only 7 years to exhaust.

The mining started at the easiest site near the fell bottom, working into the hillside with horizontal tunnels (adits) and throwing the spoil down into a steep cone below. As each level was worked out, so new adits were needed further up the hillside until progress had extended so far that an inclined plane had to be built over the spoil for a railway track. At last the ore was worked out and shafts had to be dug across the top to search downwards for the iron still buried within the fell.

The church at Boot provides clues about the relationships between farmers and miners. Because the church had to be central to a number of hamlets, it is half a mile away from Boot village. In its small and neat graveyard lie generations of Eskdale men (and Wasdale men, for, as we shall see later, at that time there was no church in their valley and their dead had to be carried on carts across the fell for burial). The gravestones speak only of long-lived farmers; there is no obvious mention made of miners, despite the fact that their dangerous jobs must have resulted in many deaths. So perhaps the close-knit farming community, during the period when there was a 'Klondike' at their back door, kept themselves to themselves as they had always done.

The walk
The walk takes a couple of hours.

(Opposite) **Boot as the miners of Nab Gill mine saw it from the fell-top: the deep trench is the site of the mine, now overgrown**

The route

🚶 from the A595
coast road near
Ravenglass [Eskdale
>]. From Hardknott
Pass, see Drive 1
🚂 By Classic Rail
from Ravenglass

1

2 Boot
♿ WC M 🅿 ∅

Parking can be difficult near Boot and you will have to take care not to obstruct the narrow lanes. Try to park a little distance away and walk into the hamlet, taking time to look over the thick walls into the small fields and to gaze up at the fell and the mine. Walking the 400 yds (366 m) from the Boot end of the Ravenglass and Eskdale railway is by far the best way to arrive.

Look carefully at the cottage walls and notice the lumpy surface cover of granite boulders. Then, as you cross the little stone pack-horse bridge, the gate ahead leads on to the fell. Immediately to the left are the mines and the remains of the mine buildings. It is an easy walk to the foot of the spoil heaps, where the dark red-brown 'bubbly' rock fragments are the remains of the haematite iron ore. *Please leave them alone for others to see.* The gentle path goes off up slope to the right but, if you are feeling energetic and have strong shoes, walk up

3

the incline to a point above the second spoil heap. There, in clefts in the left wall of the trench, you will find some of the haematite in place just as it condensed from the fluids that once flowed through the joints in the cooling granite nearly 400 million years ago. Again, *please leave the haematite alone* for others to enjoy.

4

Near here is an adit. You will probably be able to see the entrance amongst the spoil, but keep small children away from it.

5

At the top of the fell are the most dramatic mine workings of all: deep narrow slits hacked out down the joint planes of the granite. If you now follow the line of the wire guard fences across the fell you will be tracing the location of the iron-ore lens.

The fell-top is a good place to look out over Lakeland granite country. Unlike Dartmoor, where granite makes the high land, here it still lies mostly buried by the volcanic rocks. Thus the granite makes only the intermediate land of Harter Fell opposite, whereas the much higher land behind (the back of Coniston Old Man) is formed in volcanics.

By contrast with the granite fells, off to the left are the rugged volcanic peaks surrounding Hardknott Pass. To the right the view is over the progressively lower sandstone and limestone plains that eventually lead to the Irish Sea. Down below, Boot huddles at the foot of the fell, the church now seeming even more remote in the centre of the Esk valley among the large knolls of granite that provide shelter to the scattered houses.

6   The easiest way back to the village is down the fellside, which here is only moderately sloping, and along the old Wasdale Head pack-horse road. This is the route taken by the villagers of Wasdale when they went to church and especially when they came to bury their dead, for St Catherine's Church served both dales. As you walk along the water-washed track, imagine the solemn procession of villagers behind the cart on which the coffin lay. As likely as not on a cold winter's day, with the clouds scudding across the sky and rain pouring down as the people trudged their weary way to the church, even the nearby stream would have been against them, bursting over its banks and washing across their track.

12   The granite stream: the River Esk at Boot

Introduction
With the grandeur of the central fells at hand it is tempting to spend all the time in Eskdale looking up instead of down. However, away from the narrow congested roads lie a labyrinth of riverside paths, each with its own special character. The footpath beside the River Esk near Boot is full of

⇠ See Walk 11   splendid views, and all along it is edged with clues to the industrial past of the area.

The walks
The walks are all short and easy-going, along flat land on good paths. The direct route takes about 1½ hours.

The route
Boot: see Walk 11   The River Esk is one of Lakeland's most important rivers, draining valleys from much of Lakeland's south-west corner including the slopes of Scafell. By the time the waters reach Boot they have gathered from many tributary valleys, as did glaciers during the Ice Age. The history of the Esk valley floor is closely linked to the time when huge tongues of ice moved inexorably down from the nearby majestic peaks, joining together in a major glacier that finally pushed out beyond the western plains.

   Although the river channel is carved out of solid granite, most of the boulders strewn on the bed are lavas and ashes carried down from the central fells by a combination of ice and water. However, the river is now too feeble to do much more than shuffle these pebbles about, and they have still not moved far from where the ice left them.

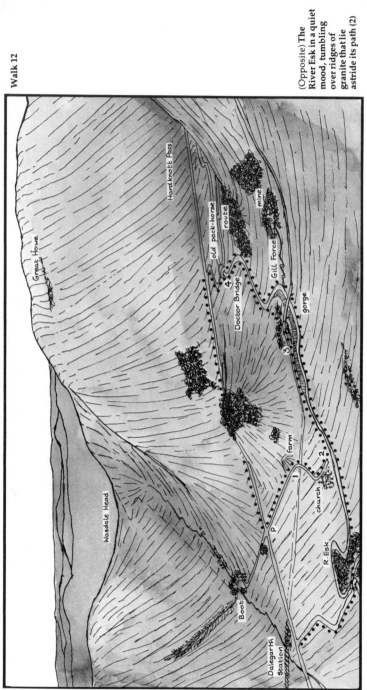

(Opposite) The River Esk in a quiet mood, tumbling over ridges of granite that lie astride its path (2)

1   The walk up the Esk begins on the floor of an old glacial valley, for the most part strewn with a bouldery clay. Only in its central stretch is it gouged down to bedrock by the melting waters of the ice. The way from Boot down to the river is enclosed in a maze of double-walled tracks just about the width of a handcart. These walls have been built from the many loose boulders that were cleared from the fields, yet, despite this, the fields remain too flat and ill drained, and the soils too heavy for use for anything but summer pasture. Notice how the farm shelters behind a part-forested knob of glacially sculptured and smoothed granite that rises, whale-backed, from the fields.

2   When you pass through the farm gate, look out for the double-walled tracks that cross your path. One of them goes left towards the Esk and the other swings towards the railway terminus. Today, abandoned and overgrown, these are remnants of past industrial activity that tell of man's use of the rocks. Remember this track: we shall meet it again further on our route.

Beside the Eskdale valley church of St Catherine, in its curiously vulnerable position alongside a flood-prone river, a broad, grassy track follows the left bank of the Esk up stream, in an area owned by the National Trust. Look down at the fine sand in the grass on the track: the river carries this over its banks in times of flood. It makes quite a contrast to the stream-bed cobbles that have been washed out of the nearby boulder clay, which are rarely moved. A little further up stream, however, you can gauge the power of the melt water, the ancestor to the present river, for here the valley narrows into a small gorge, some 20 ft (6 m) deep, through which tumble the small waterfalls of Gill Force. If you stand on the rocks that jut out into the stream, you

3   will see the deep clear pools that were drilled into the granite as this meltwater torrent swirled cobbles round and round. Today, the pools make brilliant mirrors for the fells beyond. Notice the footpath climbing an embankment towards the gorge and its extension across the gap on a bridge whose gaunt iron skeleton still stands. This is a continuation of the old walled trackway we passed earlier – a last vestige of a horse-drawn mineral railway that descended from mines in the eastern fell to join the steam railway at Boot. Here, too, you are directly opposite the iron ore that was mined at Boot.

(Opposite) **Doctor Bridge (4)**

As you move on, the land opens up again with coppiced woods on the hillside to the right. Coppicing invariably indicates the former use of forest land to produce charcoal for metal-working and its presence shows how great was the need for charcoal, because the nearest furnace was at the coast, more than 10 miles (16 km) away.

Even though the valley remains quite wide and open, notice how the fells ahead are much more craggy in appearance and very much higher than the smooth surrounding hills. Here, you are looking towards Scafell (3162 ft; 964 m) and you are on the most easterly outcrop of granite in the Esk valley, the distant fells being made of volcanic rocks.

4   Doctor Bridge over the Esk is one of Lakeland's famous stone pack-horse bridges, built where granite rises to the surface on both banks in an area where otherwise boulder clay provides unsure footings. Today, the bridge connects one isolated farmhouse with the main road, yet its site and size suggest that it was once more important. In fact, along the river all the way from St Catherine's Church, we have followed a pack-horse route, now discarded in favour of the all-weather motor route. The motor route cannot be seen from the river, because the Esk valley is split by a granite hill that resisted even the abrasive attack of ice. The road follows a virtually streamless higher gap, which must have been carved by ice, and it gives a gentle and direct descent to the starting point.

⌑ Woolpack Inn up valley on main road

Either return on the far bank to cross the Esk again at Dalegarth (and the railway station) *or* return by the road

13   Skirting the Old Man: the Walna Scar road, Coniston

Introduction

Coniston Old Man is one of the best known and most climbed of the Lakeland fells. Together with Dow Crag it makes a final southerly salient of high fell and from its summit you can look out for tens of miles to the Irish Sea with no high fells to block the view. The broad back of the Old Man allows small children and energetic grandparents to reach the summit and return in a day, but a much quieter and equally scenic route follows the lower slopes that skirt the higher fell summits. This is the Walna Scar road, an old pack-horse trail built to connect Coniston with the coast at Ravenglass. This trail may even have been in use in Roman times, and was certainly used for hundreds of years as a summer route across a low gap in the fells.

No one faced with a journey on foot, leading heavily laden horses, is going to climb more than is absolutely necessary, nor deviate from the most direct course. In consequence, the Walna Scar 'road' is remarkably straight and level, a masterpiece of route-finding across difficult terrain.

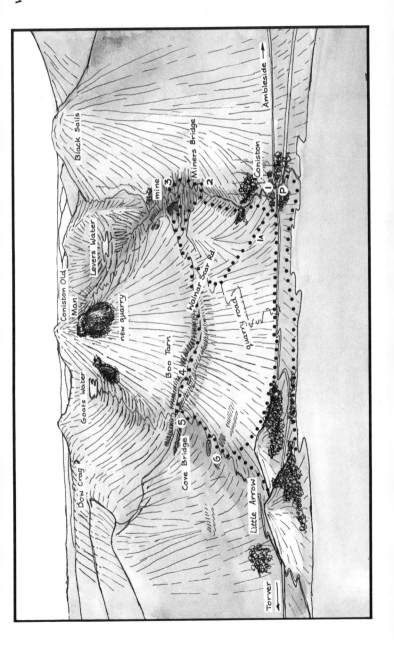

The walks

(a) Short and moderately easy with good views. Follow **1a,4** and return (about 1½ hours).

(b) Longer but with very little more uphill effort. Follow **1** through to **6**. Much of a day: take a packed lunch.

The route

⚓ Coniston, near Ambleside: Coniston
[PO] [P] WC 🍽 🏠 ⏣ M

Coniston is a small village standing some way back from the lake. It was the home of John Ruskin and was later made world famous by Donald Campbell as he tried to break the world water-speed record in the 1950s and '60s. Standing on the bridge in the middle of Coniston you see not a bustling tourist resort but a quiet stone-built village of a few shops, and a scatter of cottages, with a few hotels and inns for visitors. Unlike Ambleside, Coniston has not

Route **1a** walk south along main road, beyond garage right [Walna Scar road >]

grown. This may be because it is not as centrally placed in Lakeland, but perhaps also because it turns its back on the lake.

Coniston was not built beside the lake, because the lake shore is very low-lying and mostly marshy. Below the village, too, the small beck flowing beneath the bridge dumps the debris it has carried from the fellsides to make a small delta. The bridging point is therefore squeezed between the high fell and marshy delta, and this has determined the site of Coniston – the place on which local lakeside routes temporarily converged, and a travellers' rest.

Route **1** walk up hill to Sun Inn [Coniston Old Man >]

A lakeside route is not the best in this difficult upland country, for there are many marshy areas and stream deltas to cross. Sometimes it has proved better to choose a higher, drier site. Indeed, the gap of Yewdale leading from Ambleside in the north even directs travellers away from the lake. In the past, pack-horse track, road and railway have all avoided the lakeside and in the main they have chosen higher-level routes. Our walk will follow in the footsteps of ancient travellers who found a very useful glacially eroded trough parallel to the lakeside. It begins, appropriately for travellers, at the old Sun Inn.

The Sun Inn seems remarkably out of the way until you appreciate that the present town bridge

---

(Opposite) **The Coppermines Youth Hostel at the foot of the rise to the Old Man summit: the route along the Walna Scar goes left across the stream**

is only the most recent of many predecessors. In earlier times the normal way across the fells passed the Inn and provided considerable custom.

The Coniston fells were just as severely glaciated as any other part of Lakeland and they have the bowl-shaped combes and tarns to prove it. On crossing the field beyond the inn, look up above the forest ahead. You are confronted with what appears to be an impenetrable wall of rock, with craggy fells to left and right. Do not be dismayed at the prospect of a stiff climb, because the perspective foreshortens the view and the path is really quite easy. In fact you are looking at the side of the glaciated valley, which is still partly filled by Coniston Water.

Ahead, between the fells, there is a low gap, almost semi-circular in profile. This, too, is a glaciated valley and we are looking at it in cross 2 section, for it has been left 'hanging' high up on the fell because the glacier that eroded it was too small to compete with the scouring action of the giant neighbour that created the rock basin for Coniston Water. There are several waterfalls and rapids within this hanging valley. In the valley you can also catch a glimpse of the dams and other devices installed to direct the stream waters, for now you are near to another part of Coniston's history – its mines.

Once you have left the woods the track is gentler and the valley appears to widen into a large U shape, because this is the floor of the hanging valley. Notice how the bottom of the valley is flat, and how gently the river flows across its boulder-strewn floor. Here, just beyond Miners Bridge, you will probably be struck by the tremendous view opening out. At its head the valley divides into two. On the right is Red Fell, a glacial U-shaped valley with a flat floor. On the right a sheer wall leads up to Lever's Water, a rock-basin lake unseen on our present walk. Above these valleys to the left is Coniston Old Man and to the right Black Sails.

Here the works of man are almost equally as striking as the dramatic natural scenery. Directly ahead are huge piles of spoil that tell of the past search for copper ore. Try to reconstruct the long-forgotten scene. On the valley sides to the right are heaps of freshly worked rock and above each a

(Opposite) **Coniston copper-mine processing plant,** *c.*1860

small tunnel runs, through which miners push wagons filled with copper ore, into the fellside. In the centre of the view are huge piles of charcoal and copper ore from which smoke pours continually. Lower down, huge spoil heaps are constantly expanding and threaten to engulf the stone-built cottages and rough wooden huts that house the miners. Moving down the track you have just ascended are convoys of horses and mules, each with panniers laden with the refined metal, en route to Coniston for shipment south across the lake. In those days, everything would have been smoke, noise and toil, as 300 men hacked at the rich copper seams. Today, it is an eerie scene of desolation, with only the spoil heaps, a row of small cottages and the mine manager's house (now a youth hostel) as relics of the former turmoil.

3   If you look closely at the waste, you may find dull, brassy-yellow fragments of copper ore (copper pyrites) or glassy quartz hacked from the copper veins. The rest of the debris is simply a pile of ash and broken lava rock. This waste is doomed to remain as barren cones because it is toxic to plants until the weather can further break down the rock into soil. Even then, many decades of rain water will be needed before the copper has been washed out and the grass can grow once more.

On the left, above the mining area, the slate quarry is now the only surviving industry of the fell. You may well hear the dull thud of blasting operations. Our route, however, skirts the base of the Old Man and strikes out across an unusually level strip of land that runs around the fellside, part of the Walna Scar road. As you walk along the grassy track you will notice how well chosen the route is. In a landscape full of steep slopes and marshy hollows, the 'road' picks its way along the side of a natural level channel that lies obliquely across the fellside, providing the pack-horse driver or the cattle drover with the added bonus of magnificent views out over Coniston Water.

Return to Miners Bridge, cross, go up slope [Old Man >]. On brow of hill turn left across fell until you meet the quarry road. Follow road down hill to [Walna Scar road >] then turn right

How is it possible for a natural channel to run obliquely across the fellside when, after all, water always flows down hill? Indeed, this strange channel is already broken up by streams doing just that. The best place to unravel the mystery is to the left of the reedy Boo Tarn, where you can look both ways along the channel. Ahead it runs towards the great 'bite' out of the fellside, which is Walna Scar;

4   behind you it leads back towards the mines. Paradoxically, this cannot be the work of normal run-

ning water, yet the channel *has* been cut by a river: a river confined under ice. Although glaciers are solid ice, each summer their surfaces melt and the meltstreams disappear down great vertical cracks (crevasses) before carving ice tunnels in the depths of the glacier. The great weight of ice, however, keeps the glacier firmly held down on to the rock floor, restricting the scope of these torrents but giving them added force because of the enormous confining pressure. On many occasions, streams are forced to flow not directly down the valley side but nearly horizontally. At Boo Tarn you are standing in a trench cut into solid rock by just such a stream. After the Ice Age was over, the drainage on the fells returned to normal. Hillside streams once more flowed directly down hill, cutting across the glacially influenced channel. One stream that cuts a particularly deep gash across the channel is Torver Beck. This is crossed by Cove Bridge, a stone bridge with an iron railing. A few yards below the bridge the beck cascades into the gaping hole of a flooded slate quarry. Just above and to the right of the quarry is a broad, low mound of soil, reminding us that these fells have been inhabited for thousands of years. The mound – called a tumulus – is the burial tomb of a Bronze Age chief dating perhaps from 1000 BC. However, this chief and his clan would have seen not the open treeless fellside of today, but thin woodland. It is the more recent sheep farming that has produced the open grazing land we take to be Lakeland's 'natural' vegetation. Indeed, it is worth looking around at the few remaining lone trees. If these can survive, so could a forest, if the saplings were not continually eaten by sheep.

At main road turn left to return direct to Coniston, *or* go right then left down lane then left on footpath to lakeside. Return via lake shore to Coniston

The quarry area offers the last broad views of lake and fell, because the return journey across slaty rocks passes through hedged fields and patchy woodland down to the hamlet of Little Arrow and the road back to Coniston.

14 The edge of Britain: St Bees Head

Introduction

Many seem to think that Lakeland is far from the coast, so it may come as a surprise to discover that not only can you see across to the Isle of Man from the fells of central Lakeland but also that it is less than 12 miles (19 km) from Lakeland's edge to the seaside. For children, who may feel that lakes and mountains are fine but a day on the beach is better,

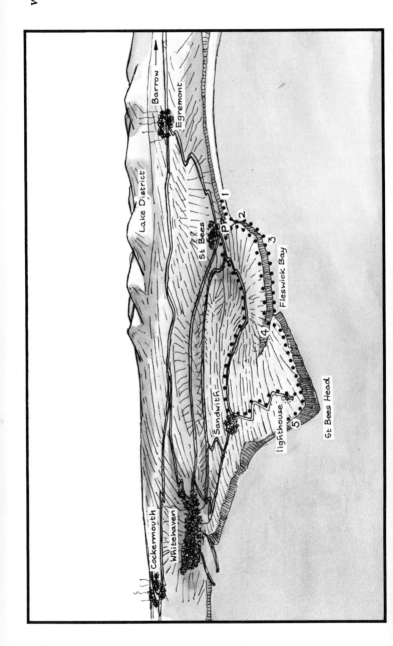

St Bees is one of the best places to go. The St Bees area is also different from the rest of the Cumbrian coast. Rather than the usual low, crumbling cliffs of so much of the north-west coast, there are towering rocky cliffs that plunge into the sea, and there is a splendid walk too.

St Bees, near Whitehaven. From Cockermouth [Egremont A5086 >] then right [St Bees >] (also British Rail)

The walks

(a) Short and easy. Follow **1,2,3** (1 hour).
(b) Longer, along the cliff-top. Follow **1,2,3 (B) 4,5** (2 hours).
(c) More adventurous, along the boulder-strewn shore at low tide. Follow **1,2,3 (A) 4,5**. Take your sandwiches and read the tide tables. Only begin the route on a falling tide and allow 2 hours for the shoreline part of the walk.

The route

The seaside walk is only part of this excursion. To appreciate the setting of St Bees, you need to understand a little about its surroundings.

For most people driving into the ancient village, all roads begin at Egremont. This is an interesting town in its own right, being the natural market centre for the western valleys of Ennerdale and Wasdale. Like Cockermouth to the north, this is a town not of the upland fell but of the lowland plain. It sits firmly on the rolling hills, whose great thickness of boulder clay, laid by retreating ice sheets, masks even the modest relief of the limestone rock beneath. As a gateway to the Lakes and an obvious route along the coast, the strategic importance of the site of Egremont was exploited by the Normans 900 years ago. Anxious to protect themselves from the marauding Scots, they built a castle whose remains still rise clear of the town and offer a good view. Except for the occasional interruptions by invaders from the north, Egremont settled down to exchanging fell sheep and cattle for bread grain and clay pots. However, the peace of this small market town was rudely interrupted when iron ore was discovered in the underlying limestone. Within a few years the sandstone-built houses forming Egremont's core were engulfed by a sea of redbrick workman's terraces as industry cast its shadow over the town.

The 19th century was the heyday of Egremont but the iron is now worked out, the jobs are gone and the town is left with a sad and somewhat faded air, as it tries to retain its life-blood light industry while still catering for tourists. The townsfolk of

Egremont and the nearby coal port of Whitehaven transformed St Bees from a quiet backwater village into a seaside town complete with hotels and promenade.

As you approach St Bees by road, you could be in Devon and a thousand miles away from coal and iron. Here, the boulder clay alternately thickens and thins to give gently rolling hills, outlined not by the stark stone walls of Lakeland but by gentle green hedges. The railway also visits St Bees on its way to the coast, although the undulating country posed some problems for the railway engineers. From the level crossing you can see clearly how they have used an old channel cut into the boulder clay by melting water at the end of the Ice Age. This enables the railway to wriggle into St Bees and out again with a minimum of cuttings and embankments.

Before the holiday-makers arrived in force, the little village of St Bees had hardly developed from the time when St Bega, an Irish saint, founded a monastery here in AD 650. The village, originally built inland away from the battering of the waves, has recently sprawled across the lower cliffs, whose low irregular profile shows all the signs of rapid
1 erosion. This is clearly not the place to build, because the cliff is made not from solid rock but from glacial boulder clay, which cannot withstand the battering of winter storms. Indeed, you have only to pick up a handful of the pebbly clay to see how easily it is removed. As you do so, see whether the pebbles are of interlocked white and black crystals of granite from Criffel mountain, away across the Solway Firth, or of the grey–green volcanic rocks from neighbouring Lakeland. As you face the cliff, you are looking at the rocks that once filled the Buttermere and Crummock Water valleys, for this is where the ice-scoured rock from Lakeland went to: it was carried on to the plain and dumped there. Now the sea is quickly removing it, and somewhere, well back from the present shore, lies the solid rock that formed the coast in the days before the Ice Age. Only when this has been finally exhumed from its boulder clay cover will the retreat of the coast slow down. In the meantime, the local authorities are trying to thwart Nature with groynes and a sea wall; the collapsing cliff is sobering evidence of their failure so far.

(Opposite) **The cliffs have been made more vulnerable to collapse because they tilt very gently towards the sea**

2 on the rocky ledge
below the red cliffs

Although the bay at St Bees may remain temporarily blocked up with boulder clay, whatever glacial debris formerly masked the headland has long since been washed away and the solid rock is exposed once more. This allows you to see in section the brilliant red sandstones that formed in a desert over 200 million years ago. Here, too, the power of the sea is evident: at the cliff base is a rocky ledge marking the retreat of even this hard material since the end of Ice Age times.

Graffiti usually despoil rocks, but here they are carefully carved works of art, some very old. Note how the more recently dated graffiti are still sharp edged whereas those near the water line and 140 years old are becoming illegible – a measure of the speed of rock weathering.

Most rocks along this coast are not sculptured simply by the action of the water, because water, like ice, needs tools to accomplish the task. Near the bay there are many rounded pebbles, which, in times of storm, are repeatedly thrown against the cliffs. Out on the headland there are only large, immovable boulders, and here the waves are constantly driven into cracks in the rock, acting like a power wedge. Slowly but surely, rocks near the water-line are dragged from the cliff by this wedging process, leaving the material above without support and prone to collapse. All the boulders on the beach beneath the headland cliffs came from such cliff falls.

3

The headland is an intricate maze of caves and rock pillars, showing the way in which the sea is undercutting the land. It is helped by the jointed nature of the sandstone and by the belts of shattered rock formed millions of years ago when earthquakes shook the area and whole chunks of the Earth's crust scraped past one another.

Either go along the
cliff-top path or
continue along the
foreshore. Be
prepared for a lot of
'boulder hopping'.
Only go on a *falling*
tide. At Fleswick Bay
take the cliff-top
path

Fleswick Bay is an enclave within the main headland mass partly eroded along the fault line. The fault has also determined the course of the small stream that tumbles into the bay. Fleswick Bay also has a rocky, wave-cut ledge that looks just like an egg box – the result of rock being attacked by the sea along its cracks: the cores of the blocks remain upstanding while the cracks are slowly widened. Behind this platform lies a small shingle beach.

4

(Opposite) **Egg-box shapes sculpted by the waves at Fleswick Bay**

5 RSPB sanctuary: colonies of guillemots, fulmars, razorbills and kittiwakes

The coast between St Bees Head and Fleswick Bay is more easily seen from the cliff-top path; moreover, along this path there are viewing points. Near the lighthouse you can look across the cliff and see daylight through great yawning cracks where another large block of rock is about to fall. The edge is no place for man, so keep to the path!

From St Bees Head to beyond the lighthouse the view unfolds to show the whole Cumbrian coast and the Solway coast of Scotland. Far on the horizon is the broad swell of Criffell mountain near Dumfries; nearer at hand the smoke from Workington's chimneys can often be seen. The nearby harbour, however, belongs to the once-famous and important town of Whitehaven.

Looking towards Whitehaven from St Bees you will notice how the coastal rock is no longer deep red but a pale yellow colour. Between here and Whitehaven the red desert sandstone disappears and the cliffs are carved instead from the sands of an ancient sea delta. If you go down to the sea beyond here, you will, in fact, find yellow rocks alternating with brown rocks made from coastal swamp muds. It was in these coastal swamps that tropical trees were buried and compressed into coal. Near St Bees you see a cross section through the type of rocks in which all Britain's coal reserves are found.

Coal formed the basis of Whitehaven's prosperity for two centuries. Below the town lie a maze of abandoned galleries and shafts. Today, only the Haig colliery perches on the cliff-top, the profile of its winding gear and chimneys a memory of the former success of the region. Viewed from the hill above the town, it is not only the colliery that dominates the skyline, but also the chimneys (and, at the cliff foot, the waste!) of a quite different industry. Although the red desert sandstones are mostly useless to industry, within them lie valuable salt deposits, the remains of great desert salt lakes. Today, these salts form the basis of a more modern industry – chemicals. Yet even before these resources were discovered, the Romans realised that because St Bees Head is the only headland for tens of miles either way, it is a splendid place for a watch-tower. The lighthouse now serves just about the opposite purpose to that of the old Roman watch-tower, yet both rely on the resistance of desert sandstones for their superb vantage point.

Return along the coastal path or go inland by the lighthouse and return by country lanes

A classic journey by steam train from Ravenglass to Eskdale

Introduction

The commercial history of the Ravenglass and Eskdale railway (known as 'Ratty') must be one of Britain's shortest. The entire system is but an obscure branch line tucked away in a remote part of the Lakeland fells and only 7 miles (11.3 km) long. It was commercially viable for only 7 years, which makes its survival all the more remarkable. Perhaps it is the obscurity that fascinates, or simply the wonder at the great natural obstacles that the railway builders had to overcome. There is the added interest of the struggle of the miners as they worked in appalling conditions to win the precious cargo the railway had been built to carry. Today, however, the real attraction for many is quite different: it is the chance to capture the flavour of a journey by steam train and at the same time to sample part of Lakeland's picturesque granite scenery. 'Ratty' provides a relaxing alternative to driving on crowded roads, and gives a unique perspective on the landscape.

It was the Cumberland iron-making boom of the 1860s and '70s that drew people looking for new sources of ore to Lakeland. At the time, Cumberland ore was the only suitable source of steel and its high prices made economic the exploitation of even remote reserves, in spite of difficult conditions in the mines, and a specially built railway. At its peak, over 8000 tons of very pure ore was won from the narrow seam of Nab Gill mine near Boot each year. However, the venture relied entirely on the monopoly of Cumberland ore, and when new methods of making steel with any type of iron ore came into use in 1879, the price of Cumberland ore slumped overnight. After a mere 7 years in production, the Boot mines and the railway were doomed.

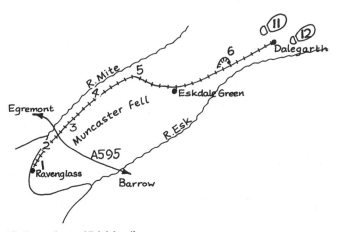

The Ravenglass and Eskdale railway

By steam train from Ravenglass to Eskdale 153

The first railway was of 3-foot gauge, designed specifically to carry ore wagons on a single track using a limited number of passing places. However, the owners also had an eye on the increasing potential traffic from tourists eager to get close to the foot of Scafell. To cater for these people, a passenger carriage was added to the ore trucks on some journeys. It must have been a fascinating sight as the tourists in their tweeds or long skirts disembarked amongst the noise of steam pumps, crushing hammers and all the activity of iron mining at Boot. Yet the tourists' traffic was never anything but a small bonus for the railway owners and when the iron mining collapsed there was an urgent need for an alternative use for the railway. After decades of decay the 3-foot gauge was finally ripped up in the 1920s and replaced with a 15-inch miniature gauge – a toy railway on a massive scale. These 'toy' trains were powerful enough to perform commercial tasks. With an increasing demand for granite as kerbstones and for road metal, the engines were again provided with trucks, and quarrying became a mainstay of this new railway. However, the expense of quarrying in this remote area was eventually too great and the railway once more passed into decline. Finally, some 20 years ago, the whole track was rescued by the Ravenglass and Eskdale Railway Preservation Society. It is on the restored track that thousands of tourists complete their classic rail journey today, pulled by smart miniature steam and diesel engines and carried in specially designed open or closed carriages.

The route

The return journey to Boot takes nearly 2 hours, including a half-hour break at Dalegarth (Boot) station. Trains run every half hour in the holiday season. However, there is so much to see at Boot (see Walks 11 and 12) that it is wise to allow a whole day, taking one train up in the morning, walking, having a picnic or a pub lunch and then returning in the late afternoon. There is adequate parking at Ravenglass.

⟵ Ravenglass is on the main A595 (T) coast road between Egremont and Grange-over-Sands 🚉 beside British Rail station

From Ratty 🅿, take time to walk to the village. Allow 1 hour. Ravenglass 🅿 ∅ 🅿🅾 WC ♿

The ride

1 Ravenglass, on the River Esk estuary, has provided a natural sheltered port for small boats since the time of the Romans. Here, a Roman garrison built the fort of Glavioventa and small boats are still drawn up on to the sands. A walk through the village soon sets the scene – a small fishing village whose life must have been severely disrupted when coastal iron carriers began to use the port to take Eskdale ore to far-off steel works. Today, Ravenglass has reverted to its rôle as a small, isolated village set behind protective sand dunes.

The enormous expanse of mudflats and sand dunes is partly the work of the River Esk washing

(Opposite) **The Eskdale railway near Dalegarth**

material down from Lakeland, and partly the result of erosion of the nearby soft cliffs of boulder clay. In this sheltered area there is simply too much material for the sea to carry away, so here it lies, leaving Ravenglass a full mile from the open sea and with no chance of becoming a significant modern port.

Ratty never depended significantly on coastal ships to carry away its iron ore. Rather, it transferred its cargoes to standard-gauge trucks on the main coastal railway line. Indeed, it is from the main-line junction that Ratty branches out inland, leaving the coast behind and heading for the fells.

The route chosen for the line follows not the wide, marshy valley of the Esk but the smaller, slightly higher and less marshy valley that runs to the north, tracking first along the edge of the estuary and then across the lowest slopes of the 2 granite of Muncaster Fell. On the left the low skyline is dominated by the sand dunes lining the coast as far as the power station at Calder Hall.

At Muncaster Mill station there is a restored 3 water-powered corn-mill driven by a leat (artificial channel), whose source is crossed over a mile further on. With insufficient water available on the fell, a more reliable source was needed, so this is a mill powered not by cascading water from the fells but by water taken from a lowland river.

Although the railway line follows a lowland route, its destination at Boot station is some 150 ft (46 m) higher than Ravenglass. Taking this into account, the railway engineers designed the track to allow it to gain height as steadily as possible, while keeping to the narrow strip of land between the poor foundation material of the boulder-clay plain and the craggy, steep fellside. You can easily detect the changing gradient by the labouring sound of the engine.

The whole of Muncaster Fell was scoured by 4 glaciers in the Ice Age, leaving it stark and barren. In the cold climate that followed the retreat of the ice, huge blocks of granite were prised free by frost and now litter the lower slopes. Only slowly is the fellside gaining a soil and plant cover, and at present few trees have managed to colonise the upper slopes, leaving only bracken to soften the scene.

Granite boulders were not confined to the slopes of Muncaster Fell. Many were brought down from Lakeland by glaciers and dumped haphazardly where people later decided to farm. The stone walls

Overshadowed by Boot Fell, 'Ratty' reaches its terminus at Dalegarth station

you pass, made with boulders taken from the fields, are not just to confine animals: they were also a useful way of clearing the ground.

5   Just before Irton Road station at the hamlet of Eskdale Green, Muncaster Fell gives way to a more open stretch of ice-scoured rocks and you see the first view of the Esk valley. The village of Eskdale, like the railway, is well off the irregular valley floor with its boggy stretches, keeping to the drier site of the saddle through which the railway has just passed.

    From now on, the line hugs the other side of the granite fell, keeping high ground on the left and again seeking a path just off the wet valley floor. Here the landscape is more dramatic, with steep knobbly crags not only above but also across the valley. Clearly, we are entering the typical scenery of Lakeland's fells. As the railway keeps hard against the fellside, you can see the pink granite

6 very clearly. Almost immediately afterwards you will see the River Esk to your right. Just ahead and to the left of the track is one of the great granite quarries, now almost hidden from sight by thickets.

    On this final stretch of the track the railway engineers must have found it increasingly difficult to avoid the upstanding knolls of tough granite and would have been forced to cut through them.

By steam train from Ravenglass to Eskdale   157

Glaciers have also scraped and plucked at the granite, leaving a smoothed side facing the direction from which the ice came, and a rougher, plucked side at the end most protected from its direct abrasive force. Look closely at all the rocky outcrops and, even if you did not know that the high fells were ahead, you can easily tell that ice moved down Eskdale.

Beyond Beckfoot the track keeps to a narrow bench above the valley, providing a view right up into the ice-scoured valley of Eskdale beyond Dalegarth station and Boot. The famous mine of Nab Gill lies in the fell just ahead, a narrow vein of iron for which this entire railway was built. Despite its importance, little shows on the surface. Its position is, unfortunately, only clear when you know where to look, so at the terminus visit Boot Fell and the mine.

Dalegarth ☕:
Walks 11, 12

CUCKOO

The cuckoo is perhaps Britain's most notorious bird because of the way it lays its eggs in other birds' nests, forcing them to rear its young. However, it is a shy woodland bird that is often heard but seldom seen. A summer visitor to Britain, the cuckoo is a large, slightly plump grey bird with dark and light grey bars across its breast.

Appendix: other useful information

Within reach of Kendal

Kendal: shopping; castle; park; Castle Dairy Museum; Abbot Hall Art Gallery; Museum of Lakeland Life and Industry; Kendal Borough Museum; Sizergh Castle (National Trust) 3 miles (5 km) south near A6/A51 junction; Levens Hall 5 miles (8 km) south of Kendal on the A6 (house and model steam engines); Heron Corn-mills, Beetham, near Milnthorpe (restored and working); Leighton Hall, Yealand (furniture, doll's house, birds of prey); Steamtown Railway Museum, Carnforth; Cartmel Priory Gatehouse, 5 miles (8 km) south of Newby Bridge (National Trust); Lakeside and Haverthwaite steam railway at southern end of Windermere.

Within reach of Ambleside and Windermere

Windermere: shopping; Bowness, ferry to Hawkshead and Belle Island, Steamboat Museum; boat trips on the lake.
Ambleside: shopping; Townend, Troutbeck, 17th century farmhouse (National Trust); Lake District National Park Centre, Brockhole, on A591 between Ambleside and Windermere: house, gardens, information, demonstrations; Grasmere, church and village; Dove Cottage and Wordsworth Museum (on A591); Rydal Mount (Wordsworth's last home); Wordsworth daffodil fields, Rydal (Dora's Field). Near Elterwater: slate works, Skelwith Force; home of Beatrix Potter (Hill Top) near Sawrey (National Trust) on west bank of Windermere lake via Hawkshead ferry; Hawkshead Courthouse (National Trust), Museum of Wildlife; Grizedale Forest Visitor and Wildlife Centre (Forestry Commission), south-west of Hawkshead on Satterthwaite road (displays, forest walks).
Near Coniston: Ruskin Museum, Coniston, and Ruskin's home, Brantwood, on east bank of Coniston Water.

Within reach of Eskdale

Swarthmoor Hall, Ulverston (birthplace of Quakerism); Dalton Castle, Dalton-in-Furness (National Trust); Furness Abbey between Barrow and Dalton (DOE); Furness museum, Barrow-in-Furness; Viking/Saxon church at Gosforth, near Wasdale; Muncaster Mill (restored corn-mill); Muncaster Castle and grounds. *Ravenglass:* Roman Fort at Ravenglass; Millom Folk Museum; Wastwater Screes, Wasdale; Egremont Castle and park.

Within reach of Keswick

Keswick: shopping; Moot Hall Museum; boat trips on lake; Fitz Park Museum and Art Gallery; Whinlatter Pass Visitor Centre near Braithwaite (Forestry Commission): includes displays and forest trails; Castlerigg stone circle above Keswick on A591 to Ambleside; stone circle near Threkeld on A6 to Penrith road; Bowder Stone (glacial erratic), Borrowdale near Lodore falls; Dacre Castle, north end of Ullswater.

Tourist information centres

Ambleside: Information Centre. Tel. Ambleside 2582
Barrow-in-Furness: Civic Hall. Tel. Barrow 25795
Cockermouth: Riversdale Car Park. Tel. Cockermouth 2634
Egremont: Main Street. Tel. Egremont 820693
Kendal: Town Hall. Tel. Kendal 23649
Keswick: Moot Hall. Tel. Keswick 72803
Ravenglass: steam railway station. Tel. Ravenglass 278
Windermere: beside railway station. Tel. Windermere 4561

The Cumbria Tourist Board: Ellerthwaite, Windermere LA23 2AQ